目　錄

特別的感謝

2002學年度會長　　　：徐永生　　　副會長：李昭育　　　　　秘書長：宋貞
教育委員會召集人：許玲瑤、方治欽、林蓮華
老師：程淑慧、沈淑瓊、汪星潔、林秀娟、張榕君、余春櫻、陳淑娟、易雲美
　　　黃瑞齡、李筱萍、項亞珍、黃慧君、楊大蓉、林渝華、龍瑞蘭、林念萱
　　　金淑秀、劉麗銂

2001學年度會長　　　：黃楷棋
教育委員會召集人：許玲瑤、方治欽、林蓮華
老師：沈淑瓊、黃慧君、金淑秀、光若蘋、易雲美、余春櫻、楊大蓉、項亞珍
　　　張榕君、柯瑞瑄

2000學年度會長　　　：孫燕福
教育委員會召集人：方治欽、吳士寧、張方中
老師：沈淑瓊、黃慧君、茅爲洵、光若蘋、龍瑞蘭、莫兆鳳、羅梅蓉、劉麗銂
　　　陳台昆、張榕君、周均

1999學年度會長　　　：艾力
教育委員會召集人：徐永生、方治欽、郭美玲
老師：沈淑瓊、金淑秀、吳美慧、李秋丹、許錫珍、賀珊珊、陳台昆、羅梅蓉
　　　張榕君、姜新新、陳淑娟、葉賽儂、周均

1998學年度會長　　　：高玉麗
教育委員會召集人：孫燕福、方治欽、柯錦忠
老師：姜愛玲、楊大蓉、易雲美、余春櫻、鄭淑琴、李漢雯、王美珠、許錫珍
　　　金淑秀

SAT II 中文測驗説明

一、 考試時間

SAT II Chinese每年只考一次，通常是在十一月初的週末考試。考生可在九月份向所讀高中索取報名表。相關資料請在www.collegeboard.com查詢。

二、 考試範圍

SAT II中文測驗的目的是衡量你對中文的瞭解以及在日常生活中的溝通能力。由於美國的外語教學非常注重學生對生活語言的實際應用能力。所以SAT II中文測驗的內容也不例外，都是和日常生活的食衣住行娛樂有關。

三、 考試方式

SAT II中文測驗考試一共有85道選擇題，時間是一個小時。其中三部分：聽力（30題）佔20分鐘、語法（25題）和閱讀（30題）佔40分鐘。

聽力部分的考題是用錄音帶播出，考卷上沒有文字。這一部分的題目是用簡短的對話或敘述日常生活裡的一件事來測驗你聽中文的能力。在錄音帶中每一道題目只説一次。所以你要集中注意力去聽。然後圈選考卷上最正確的答案。

語法部份是用一般生活中使用的語句來測驗你是否能正確使用中文字彙和文法。每一題都分別以正體字、簡化字、漢語拼音及注音符號四種型態列出。考生只須用你最擅長熟悉的一種來作答就可以。

閱讀部份是用你平常生活中可能遇到的真實情況為考題。其中包括便條、信件、時刻表、日記、新聞報導、招牌、菜單、天氣預報…等。這些題目是用中文的正體或簡體兩種形式印出。考生只要看懂其中一種就可以。所有題目都是用英文來問，全部都是選擇題。

四、 攜帶用品（Cassette Players）

你必須自己攜帶一個可以被接受的錄音機（附帶有耳機）到考場。最好是在考前先換上一個新的電池。你也可以多準備一套備用的錄音機。考試中心是不提供電池、錄音機或耳機的。

五、計分方式

正式考試的總分是用200-to-800的 score 來統計。而聽力、語法和閱讀的小統計則是用20-to-80的 score 來計算，請參考Collegeboard公佈的計算表來計算。在本書的模擬測驗中，請用本書後面所附上的模擬試題答案卷（Answer Sheet）來作答，並計算你的成績。計算方法如下：

Raw Score Calculation

- The full score is <u>85 pts.</u>
- Each correct answer is <u>1 pts.</u>
- Each wrong answer for question #1.....#15 will have negative point of <u>-1/2 pts.</u>
- Each wrong answer for question #16...#85 will have negative point of <u>-1/3 pts.</u>

Reported Score Conversion Table:

Due to various factors and levels of difficulty of the real test, ANCCS doesn't use the Reported Score. The following table is only used for your reference.

Raw Score	Report Score
84	800
80	750<
74	720<
70	700<

Raw Score	Report Score
62	660<
51	600<
41	550<
31	500<

Raw Score	Report Score
23	460<
12	400<
4	360<

SAT II 中文模擬試卷 第一套
Section I : Listening Comprehension

Part A

Directions: In this part of the test you will hear short questions, statements, or exchanges in Mandarin Chinese, follow by three responses designated (A), (B), and (C). You will hear the statements or questions, as well as the responses, just one time and they are not printed in your test booklet. Therefore, you must listen very carefully. Select the best response and fill in the corresponding oval on your answer sheet. You will have 15 seconds to answer each question.

Question 1 (A) (B) (C)

Question 2 (A) (B) (C)

Question 3 (A) (B) (C)

Question 4 (A) (B) (C)

Question 5 (A) (B) (C)

Question 6 (A) (B) (C)

Question 7 (A) (B) (C)

Question 8 (A) (B) (C)

Question 9 (A) (B) (C)

Question 10 (A) (B) (C)

Question 11 (A) (B) (C)

Question 12 (A) (B) (C)

Question 13 (A) (B) (C)

Question 14 (A) (B) (C)

Question 15 (A) (B) (C)

Part B

Directions: You will now hear a series of short selections. You will hear them <u>only once</u> and they are not printed in your test booklet. After each selection, you will be asked one or more questions about what you have just heard. These questions, with four possible answers, are printed in your test booklet. Select the best answer to each question from among the four choices given and fill in the corresponding oval on your answer sheet. You will have 15 seconds to answer each question.

16~17

Question 16   Usually when she goes on vacation, what does she not bring back?

    (A)   postcard

    (B)   regional food

    (C)   T-shirt

    (D)   souvenier

Question 17   What country did she just come back from?

    (A)   England

    (B)   Italy

    (C)   France

    (D)   Germany

18

Question 18   What was the discount on this brand of shoes?

    (A)   30% off

    (B)   40% off

    (C)   50% off

    (D)   70% off

19~20

Question 19   How many required courses is he taking next semester?

    (A)   3

    (B)   4

    (C)   5

    (D)   not decided yet

Question 20   Which of the following electives is he taking next semester?

(A)   ceramics

(B)   choir

(C)   art

(D)   woodshop

21~22

Question 21   What are they concerned about?

(A)   not being able to get tickets for the game

(B)   not having transportation to the game

(C)   it might rain

(D)   their parents won't let them go to the game

Question 22   What do they want to watch?

(A)   a movie

(B)   the basketball championship game

(C)   the soccer championship game

(D)   the waterpolo championship game

23~24

Question 23   What is a possible side effect of the medication?

(A)   stomach pains

(B)   dizziness

(C)   nausea

(D)   dry mouth

Question 24   How many pills is the man supposed to take per day?

(A)   1

(B)   2

(C)   3

(D)   4

 # 25

Question 25   What does the man order?

    (A)   not decided yet

    (B)   a special combination for four persons

    (C)   four dishes

    (D)   some special dishes recommended by waiter

 # 26

Question 26   What did the woman decide on doing?

    (A)   borrow somebody's pen

    (B)   buy a new pen

    (C)   go home and get her pencil box

    (D)   ask the teacher for a pen

 # 27

Question 27   Why is the man angry?

    (A)   Nobody came to clean up his room.

    (B)   He was woken up by noises next door.

    (C)   A phone call woke him up.

    (D)   The maid came in to clean up and woke him.

 # 28

Question 28   What are the twenty dollars for?

    (A)   a jacket

    (B)   a key chain

    (C)   a backpack

    (D)   a safety deposit for a locker

 # 29

Question 29   Which of the following electricity-saving methods was not mentioned in the conversation?

(A)   replace the old refrigerator

(B)   turn off lights when not needed

(C)   start using energy-saving light bulbs

(D)   do not use electronics until after 7:00 pm

 # 30

Question 30   Why is her car missing?

(A)   It was stolen.

(B)   She can't remember where she parked.

(C)   Her car was towed away, because she parked in a private parking space.

(D)   Her car was towed away, because she double parked.

SAT II 中文模擬試題 第一套
Section I : Listening Comprehension

Part A

Directions: In this part of the test you will hear short questions, statements, or exchanges in Mandarin Chinese, followed by three responses designated (A), (B), and (C). You will hear the statements or questions, as well as the responses, just one time and they are not printed in your test booklet. Therefore, you must listen very carefully. Select the best response and fill in the corresponding oval on your answer sheet. You will have 15 seconds to answer each question.

Question 1

你這次的法文考得如何？

    (A) 還不錯。

    (B) 法文不好學。

    (C) 文法不太對。

Question 2

喂！我是陳大中的媽媽，他今天不太舒服，想請假。

    (A) 他這次假期玩得不太舒服。

    (B) 好的，他是幾年級的學生？

    (C) 他要外出旅行，想請三天假。

Question 3

我覺得這條裙子一點也不難看。

    (A) 這條裙子不好看。

    (B) 很難才找到這條裙子。

    (C) 是啊！這條裙子還不錯。

Question 4

萬一你明天早上九點不能來，請早點通知我。
    (A)好，明天早上我把錢送去給你。
    (B)好，早上九點一起去吃早點。
    (C)好，如果不能去，我儘早告訴你。

Question 5

這是單行道，你開反了，好危險！
    (A)噢！我開錯了方向。
    (B)有人開車撞到我。
    (C)我沒注意到旁邊有人騎單車。

Question 6

這個地方恰好可以放一個書架。
    (A)到哪裏買書架比較好？
    (B)那家店賣的書架很好看。
    (C)真好！這些書就有地方放了。

Question 7

公共汽車一天才五班，我們還是租車吧！
    (A)上一班公共汽車才開走。
    (B)我贊成，租車方便多了。
    (C)這條街有五條不同路線的公共汽車。

Question 8

不要緊張，時間還早，來得及去接小孩。
    (A)快來不及接小孩了。
    (B)聊得忘了時間。
    (C)不急，還有很多時間。

Question 9

上個週末天氣很反常，冷得半死，還好這個週末氣溫回升了。

(A) 上個週末很熱。

(B) 上個週末有人冷死了。

(C) 這個週末比上個週末暖和。

Question 10

A：我不太會游泳，你教我好嗎？

B：沒問題，你想學什麼式？

(A) 我試試回答這些問題。

(B) 這些問題我都不會，請你教我，好嗎？

(C) 自由式。

Question 11

銀行在中山路和第一街的交叉路口。

(A) 中山路和第一街是十字形的。

(B) 中山路和第一街是平行的。

(C) 銀行不在第一街也不在中山路上。

Question 12

抱歉！路上碰到修路，只好繞道，所以才會遲到半個鐘頭。

(A) 車子碰到磚頭，送去修理。

(B) 因為多繞了一段路才會晚到。

(C) 這個鐘壞了，不知道要送到哪裏去修理。

Question 13

這條街偶數的房子在右邊，奇數的在左邊。

    (A) 9號的房子在右邊。

    (B) 12號的房子在右邊。

    (C) 6號的房子在左邊。

Question 14

你要搭國際航線班機，拿了登機證以後，就可以到免稅商店去買東西。

    (A) 我想搭你的車子去商店買東西。

    (B) 機場的免稅商店只有搭國際航線的旅客才能進去。

    (C) 你想買什麼東西，請先登記一下。

Question 15

最近油價一直在上漲，這部老爺車很費油，換一部省油的車吧！

    (A) 這部舊車用油很兇。

    (B) 爺爺想買部新車。

    (C) 新車的價錢一直在上漲。

Part B

Directions: You will now hear a series of short selections. You will hear them only once and they are not printed in your test booklet. After each selection, you will be asked one or more questions about what you have just heard. These questions, with four possible answers, are printed in your test booklet. Select the best answer to each question from among the four choices given and fill in the corresponding oval on your answer sheet. You will have 15 seconds to answer each question.

Question 16~17

男：聽說你剛旅遊回來。

女：是啊！每次出去玩，我總會買些印有當地字樣的運動衫，紀念品和一些土產。

男：哇！好精緻的巴黎鐵塔！

女：是我這次買回來的。

Question 18

男：小姐，我要買這雙運動鞋。

女：你運氣真好，今天這個牌子的運動鞋正好打折。

男：打幾折？

女：打七折。

Question 19~20

女：下學期你選了哪些課？

男：除了英文、歷史、生物、運動等必修的五門課以外，還有陶瓷、日文兩門選修課。

女：喔！那麼重的課夠你忙的了。

Question 21~22

女：氣象報告說明天多雲偶陣雨。

男：真糟糕！明天不是高中組的足球決賽嗎？

女：是啊！今年這兩隊實力相當，不知道哪一隊會贏？

男：真希望天公能作美，不要讓我們掃興。

Question 23~24

女：這種抗生素必須飯後吃，早晚各一顆，總共要吃十天，而且一定要吃完。

男：會有什麼副作用嗎？

女：可能會頭暈，如果有這個症狀，最好不要開車。

男：好，我會按照醫生的處方吃的。

Question 25

男：介紹一下你們餐廳的招牌菜。

女：有宮保雞丁、海鮮煲、紅燒豆腐、葱爆牛肉…，招牌菜都在這張菜單裏。這一個禮拜剛好週年慶，合菜打八折，要不要試試？

男：好啊！正好在減價，又省得點菜的麻煩。

女：四人份合菜五十塊錢。

Question 26

女：糟了！我把鉛筆盒留在家裏了。

男：沒關係，跟朋友借一枝筆，或者買枝新的。

女：時間還早，還是折回去拿，裏面還有我的學生證。

Question 27

男：誰呀？怎麼回事？真倒楣！剛睡著就被吵醒。

女：對不起！我來打掃房間。你並沒有掛上「請勿打擾」的牌子，所以我才敲門。

男：喔！我以為通常下午才會來打掃。

Question 28

女：我想租個櫃子寄放東西。

男：押金二十塊錢，還鑰匙時再退還給你。

女：有沒有大一點的櫃子，我的夾克和背包都很大。

男：沒有，都一樣大。

Question 29

女：家裏的電費越來越高了。

男：大家以後要隨手關燈，也許應該改用省電燈泡了。

女：這部舊冰箱很費電，也該換了。

Question 30

女：我的車怎麼不見了？

男：這是私人停車場，你違規停車，可能被拖走了。

女：有沒有電話號碼，可以讓我問到車子的下落？

Section II : Grammar

Directions: This section consists of a number of incomplete statements, each of which has four suggested completions. Select the word or phrase that best completes the sentence structurally and logically. Please fill in the corresponding oval on the answer sheet.

THE QUESTIONS ARE PRESENTED IN FOUR DIFFERENT WRITING SYSTEMS: TRADITIONAL CHARACTERS, SIMPLIFIED CHARACTERS, PINYIN ROMANIZATION, AND CHINESE PHONETIC ALPHABET(BO PO MO FO). TO SAVE TIME, IT IS RECOMMENDED THAT YOU CHOOSE THE WRITING SYSTEM WITH WHICH YOU ARE MOST FAMILIAR WITH AND **READ ONLY THAT VERSION OF THE QUESTION.**

31. 他爲人很熱心，＿＿不認識的人，他
也會幫忙。
    - (A) 但是
    - (B) 如此
    - (C) 即使
    - (D) 除了

31. 他为人很热心，＿＿不认识的人，他
也会帮忙。
    - (A) 但是
    - (B) 如此
    - (C) 即使
    - (D) 除了

31. ㄊㄚ ㄨㄟ ㄖㄣ ㄏㄣ ㄖㄜ ㄒㄧㄣ，＿＿ㄅㄨ ㄖㄣ ㄕ ㄉㄜ ㄖㄣ，ㄊㄚ
ㄧㄝ ㄏㄨㄟ ㄅㄤ ㄇㄤ 。
    - (A) ㄉㄢ ㄕ
    - (B) ㄖㄨ ㄘ
    - (C) ㄐㄧ ㄕ
    - (D) ㄔㄨ ㄌㄜ

31. Tā wéi rén hěn rè xīn,＿＿bú rèn shì de rén, tā
yě huì bāng máng.
    - (A) dàn shì
    - (B) rú cǐ
    - (C) jí shǐ
    - (D) chú le

32. 你＿＿不知道偷東西是不好的行爲
嗎？
    - (A) 難得
    - (B) 難過
    - (C) 難道
    - (D) 難爲

32. 你＿＿不知道偷东西是不好的
行为吗？
    - (A) 难得
    - (B) 难过
    - (C) 难道
    - (D) 难为

32. ㄋㄧ ＿＿ ㄅㄨ ㄓ ㄉㄠ ㄊㄡ ㄉㄨㄥ ㄒㄧ ㄕ ㄅㄨ ㄏㄠ ㄉㄜ ㄒㄧㄥ ㄨㄟ
ㄇㄚ ？
    - (A) ㄋㄢ ㄉㄜ
    - (B) ㄋㄢ ㄍㄨㄛ
    - (C) ㄋㄢ ㄉㄠ
    - (D) ㄋㄢ ㄨㄟ

32. Nǐ ＿＿ bù zhī dào tōu dōng xi shì bù hǎo de
xíng wéi ma?
    - (A) nán dé
    - (B) nán guò
    - (C) nán dào
    - (D) nán wéi

33. 他＿＿在加州住過五年。

(A) 曾經
(B) 已經
(C) 經過
(D) 經常

33. ㄊㄚ ＿＿ㄗㄞˋㄐㄧㄚㄓㄡㄓㄨˋㄍㄨㄛˋㄨˇㄋㄧㄢˊ。

(A) ㄘㄥˊ ㄐㄧㄥ
(B) ㄧˇ ㄐㄧㄥ
(C) ㄐㄧㄥ ㄍㄨㄛˋ
(D) ㄐㄧㄥ ㄔㄤˊ

33. 他＿＿在加州住过五年。

(A) 曾经
(B) 已经
(C) 经过
(D) 经常

33. Tā ＿＿ zài Jiāzhōu zhù guò wǔ nián.

(A) céng jīng
(B) yǐ jīng
(C) jīng guò
(D) jīng cháng

34. 媽媽每天下班後，＿＿忙著做家事。

(A) 還沒
(B) 還有
(C) 還要
(D) 還給

34. ㄇㄚㄇㄚㄇㄟˇㄊㄧㄢㄒㄧㄚˋㄅㄢㄏㄡˋ，＿＿ㄇㄤˊㄓㄜ˙ㄗㄨㄛˋㄐㄧㄚㄕˋ。

(A) ㄏㄞˊ ㄇㄟˊ
(B) ㄏㄞˊ ㄧㄡˇ
(C) ㄏㄞˊ ㄧㄠˋ
(D) ㄏㄞˊ ㄍㄟˇ

34. 妈妈每天下班后，＿＿忙著做家事。

(A) 还没
(B) 还有
(C) 还要
(D) 还给

34. Mā ma měi tiān xià bān hòu, ＿＿ máng zhe zuò jiā shì.

(A) hái méi
(B) hái yǒu
(C) hái yào
(D) hái gěi

35. ＿＿我说什麼，他＿＿不相信。

(A) 不論 … 要
(B) 不要 … 都
(C) 不論 … 都
(D) 不管 … 要

35. ＿＿ㄨㄛˇㄕㄨㄛㄕㄣˊㄇㄜ˙，ㄊㄚ＿＿ㄅㄨˋㄒㄧㄤㄒㄧㄣˋ。

(A) ㄅㄨˊ ㄌㄨㄣˋ … ㄧㄠˋ
(B) ㄅㄨˊ ㄧㄠˋ … ㄉㄡ
(C) ㄅㄨˊ ㄌㄨㄣˋ … ㄉㄡ
(D) ㄅㄨˋ ㄍㄨㄢˇ … ㄧㄠˋ

35. ＿＿我说什么，他＿＿不相信。

(A) 不论 … 要
(B) 不要 … 都
(C) 不论 … 都
(D) 不管 … 要

35. ＿＿ wǒ shuō shén me, tā ＿＿ bù xiāng xìn.

(A) Bú lùn .... yào
(B) Bú yào .... dōu
(C) Bú lùn .... dōu
(D) Bù guǎn .... yào

16

36. 他____妹妹____愛彈鋼琴。

    (A) 叫…那麼

    (B) 像…爲什麼

    (C) 不像…那麼

    (D) 就像…怎麼

36. 他____妹妹____愛弹钢琴。

    (A) 叫…那么

    (B) 像…为什么

    (C) 不像…那么

    (D) 就像…怎么

36. ㄊㄚ ____ ㄇㄟˋ ㄇㄟ ____ ㄞˋ ㄊㄢˊ ㄍㄤ ㄑㄧㄣˊ。

    (A) ㄐㄧㄠˋ…ㄋㄚˋ ㄇㄜ

    (B) ㄒㄧㄤˋ…ㄨㄟˋ ㄕㄣˊ ㄇㄜ

    (C) ㄅㄨˊ ㄒㄧㄤˋ…ㄋㄚˋ ㄇㄜ

    (D) ㄐㄧㄡˋ ㄒㄧㄤˋ…ㄗㄣˇ ㄇㄜ

36. Tā ____ mèi mei ____ ài tán gāng qín.

    (A) jiào .... nà me

    (B) xiàng .... wèi shén me

    (C) bú xiàng .... nà me

    (D) jiù xiàng .... zěn me

---

37. 弟弟考得不好，被爸爸罵了一 __。

    (A) 個

    (B) 頓

    (C) 把

    (D) 合

37. 弟弟考得不好，被爸爸骂了一 __。

    (A) 个

    (B) 顿

    (C) 把

    (D) 合

37. ㄉㄧˋ ㄉㄧ ㄎㄠˇ ㄉㄜ ㄅㄨˋ ㄏㄠˇ，ㄅㄟˋ ㄅㄚˋ ㄅㄚ ㄇㄚˋ ㄌㄜ ㄧˊ __。

    (A) ㄍㄜ

    (B) ㄉㄨㄣˋ

    (C) ㄅㄚˇ

    (D) ㄏㄜˊ

37. Dì di kǎo de bù hǎo, bèi bà ba mà le yí __ .

    (A) ge

    (B) dùn

    (C) bǎ

    (D) hé

---

38. 哥哥平安地回到家，媽媽這才__。

    (A) 小心

    (B) 用心

    (C) 放心

    (D) 分心

38. 哥哥平安地回到家，妈妈这才__。

    (A) 小心

    (B) 用心

    (C) 放心

    (D) 分心

38. ㄍㄜ ㄍㄜ ㄆㄧㄥˊ ㄢ ㄉㄜ ㄏㄨㄟˊ ㄉㄠˋ ㄐㄧㄚ，ㄇㄚ ㄇㄚ ㄓㄜˋ ㄘㄞˊ __。

    (A) ㄒㄧㄠˇ ㄒㄧㄣ

    (B) ㄩㄥˋ ㄒㄧㄣ

    (C) ㄈㄤˋ ㄒㄧㄣ

    (D) ㄈㄣ ㄒㄧㄣ

38. Gē ge píng ān de huí dào jiā, mā ma zhè cái ____ .

    (A) xiǎo xīn

    (B) yòng xīn

    (C) fàng xīn

    (D) fēn xīn

39. 給他魚吃，____ 教他如何釣魚。

    (A) 不但
    (B) 不如
    (C) 不同
    (D) 不是

39. 给他鱼吃，____ 教他如何钓鱼。

    (A) 不但
    (B) 不如
    (C) 不同
    (D) 不是

39. ㄍㄟˇ ㄊㄚ ㄩˊ ㄔ，____ ㄐㄧㄠ ㄊㄚ ㄖㄨˊ ㄏㄜˊ ㄉㄧㄠˋ ㄩˊ。

    (A) ㄅㄨˊ ㄉㄢˋ
    (B) ㄅㄨˋ ㄖㄨˊ
    (C) ㄅㄨˋ ㄊㄨㄥˊ
    (D) ㄅㄨˊ ㄕˋ

39. Gěi tā yú chī, ____ jiāo tā rú hé diào yú.

    (A) bú dàn
    (B) bù rú
    (C) bù tóng
    (D) bú shì

---

40. ____ 我有翅膀，我要飛向天空。

    (A) 不但
    (B) 假如
    (C) 可以
    (D) 雖然

40. ____ 我有翅膀，我要飞向天空。

    (A) 不但
    (B) 假如
    (C) 可以
    (D) 虽然

40. ____ ㄨㄛˇ ㄧㄡˇ ㄔˋ ㄅㄤˇ，ㄨㄛˇ ㄧㄠˋ ㄈㄟ ㄒㄧㄤˋ ㄊㄧㄢ ㄎㄨㄥ。

    (A) ㄅㄨˊ ㄉㄢˋ
    (B) ㄐㄧㄚˇ ㄖㄨˊ
    (C) ㄎㄜˇ ㄧˇ
    (D) ㄙㄨㄟ ㄖㄢˊ

40. ____ wǒ yǒu chì bǎng, wǒ yào fēi xiàng tiān kōng.

    (A) Bú dàn
    (B) Jiǎ rú
    (C) Kě yǐ
    (D) Suī rán

---

41. 你要先在支票上 ____，才能提錢。

    (A) 打字
    (B) 寫字
    (C) 簽字
    (D) 造字

41. 你要先在支票上 ____，才能提钱。

    (A) 打字
    (B) 写字
    (C) 签字
    (D) 造字

41. ㄋㄧˇ ㄧㄠˋ ㄒㄧㄢ ㄗㄞˋ ㄓ ㄆㄧㄠˋ ㄕㄤˋ ____，ㄘㄞˊ ㄋㄥˊ ㄊㄧˊ ㄑㄧㄢˊ。

    (A) ㄉㄚˇ ㄗˋ
    (B) ㄒㄧㄝˇ ㄗˋ
    (C) ㄑㄧㄢ ㄗˋ
    (D) ㄗㄠˋ ㄗˋ

41. Nǐ yào xiān zài zhī piào shàng ____, cái néng tí qián.

    (A) dǎ zì
    (B) xiě zì
    (C) qiān zì
    (D) zào zì

42. 他精神很好，只 ＿＿＿ 有點累了。

    (A) 不幸

    (B) 不過

    (C) 幸好

    (D) 可惜

42. 他精神很好，只 ＿＿＿ 有点累了。

    (A) 不幸

    (B) 不过

    (C) 幸好

    (D) 可惜

42. ㄊㄚ ㄐㄧㄥ ㄕㄣ ㄏㄣ ㄏㄠ，ㄓ ＿＿＿ ㄧㄡ ㄉㄧㄢ ㄌㄟ ㄌㄜ。

    (A) ㄅㄨ ㄒㄧㄥ

    (B) ㄅㄨ ㄍㄨㄛ

    (C) ㄒㄧㄥ ㄏㄠ

    (D) ㄎㄜ ㄒㄧ

42. Tā jīng shén hěn hǎo, zhǐ ＿＿＿ yǒu diǎn lèi le.

    (A) bú xìng

    (B) bú guò

    (C) xìng hǎo

    (D) kě xí

43. ＿＿＿ 中文 ＿＿＿，我還學西班牙文。

    (A) 好像…一樣

    (B) 不但…而且

    (C) 跟著…以後

    (D) 除了…以外

43. ＿＿＿ 中文 ＿＿＿，我还学西班牙文。

    (A) 好像…一样

    (B) 不但…而且

    (C) 跟著…以后

    (D) 除了…以外

43. ＿＿＿ ㄓㄨㄥ ㄨㄣ ＿＿＿，ㄨㄛ ㄏㄞ ㄒㄩㄝ ㄒㄧ ㄅㄢ ㄧㄚ ㄨㄣ。

    (A) ㄏㄠ ㄒㄧㄤ …ㄧ ㄧㄤ

    (B) ㄅㄨ ㄉㄢ …ㄦ ㄑㄧㄝ

    (C) ㄍㄣ ㄓㄜ …ㄧ ㄏㄡ

    (D) ㄔㄨ ㄌㄜ …ㄧ ㄨㄞ

43. ＿＿＿ Zhōngwén＿＿＿, wǒ hái xué Xībānyáwén.

    (A) Hǎo xiàng .... yí yàng

    (B) Bú dàn .... ér qiě

    (C) Gēn zhe .... yǐ hòu

    (D) Chú le .... yǐ wài

44. ＿＿＿ 他離開公司以後，我們＿＿很久沒有聯絡了。

    (A) 自用…經過

    (B) 來自…經常

    (C) 自從…已經

    (D) 從來…曾經

44. ＿＿＿ 他离开公司以后，我们＿＿很久没有联络了。

    (A) 自用…经过

    (B) 来自…经常

    (C) 自从…已经

    (D) 从来…曾经

44. ＿＿＿ ㄊㄚ ㄌㄧ ㄎㄞ ㄍㄨㄥ ㄙ ㄧ ㄏㄡ，ㄨㄛ ㄇㄣ ＿＿＿ ㄏㄣ ㄐㄧㄡ ㄇㄟ ㄧㄡ ㄌㄧㄢ ㄌㄨㄛ ㄌㄜ。

    (A) ㄗ ㄩㄥ …ㄐㄧㄥ ㄍㄨㄛ

    (B) ㄌㄞ ㄗ …ㄐㄧㄥ ㄔㄤ

    (C) ㄗ ㄘㄨㄥ …ㄧ ㄐㄧㄥ

    (D) ㄘㄨㄥ ㄌㄞ …ㄘㄥ ㄐㄧㄥ

44. ＿＿＿ tā lí kāi gōng sī yǐ hòu, wǒ men ＿＿＿ hěn jiǔ méi yǒu lián luò le.

    (A) Zì yòng .... jīng guò

    (B) Lái zì .... jīng cháng

    (C) Zì cóng .... yǐ jīng

    (D) Cóng lái .... céng jīng

45. 小華的牙齒痛得 ___，連一口飯也吃
    不下。
    (A) 了不得
    (B) 不得了
    (C) 了不起
    (D) 起不了

45. 小华的牙齿痛得 ___，连一口饭也吃
    不下。
    (A) 了不得
    (B) 不得了
    (C) 了不起
    (D) 起不了

45. ㄒㄠ ㄏㄨㄚ ㄉㄜ ㄧㄚ ㄔ ㄊㄨㄥ ㄉㄜ ___，ㄌㄧㄢ ㄧ ㄎㄡ ㄈㄢ
    ㄧㄝ ㄔ ㄅㄨ ㄒㄧㄚ。
    (A) ㄌㄧㄠ ㄅㄨ ㄉㄜ
    (B) ㄅㄨ ㄉㄜ ㄌㄧㄠ
    (C) ㄌㄧㄠ ㄅㄨ ㄑㄧ
    (D) ㄑㄧ ㄅㄨ ㄌㄧㄠ

45. Xiǎohuá de yá chǐ tòng de ___, lián yì kǒu fàn
    yě chī bú xià.
    (A) liǎo bù dé
    (B) bù dé liǎo
    (C) liǎo bù qǐ
    (D) qǐ bù liǎo

46. ___，你又得了第一名。
    (A) 謝謝你
    (B) 對不起
    (C) 恭喜你
    (D) 沒問題

46. ___，你又得了第一名。
    (A) 谢谢你
    (B) 对不起
    (C) 恭喜你
    (D) 没问题

46. ___，ㄋㄧ ㄧㄡ ㄉㄜ ㄌㄜ ㄉㄧ ㄧ ㄇㄧㄥ。
    (A) ㄒㄧㄝ ㄒㄧㄝ ㄋㄧ
    (B) ㄉㄨㄟ ㄅㄨ ㄑㄧ
    (C) ㄍㄨㄥ ㄒㄧ ㄋㄧ
    (D) ㄇㄟ ㄨㄣ ㄊㄧ

46. ___, nǐ yòu dé le dì yī míng.
    (A) Xiè xie nǐ
    (B) Duì bù qǐ
    (C) Gōng xǐ nǐ
    (D) Méi wèn tí

47. 我 ___ 去過圖書館了。
    (A) 想要
    (B) 馬上
    (C) 已經
    (D) 立刻

47. 我 ___ 去过图书馆了。
    (A) 想要
    (B) 马上
    (C) 已经
    (D) 立刻

47. ㄨㄛ ___ ㄑㄩ ㄍㄨㄛ ㄊㄨ ㄕㄨ ㄍㄨㄢ ㄌㄜ。
    (A) ㄒㄧㄤ ㄧㄠ
    (B) ㄇㄚ ㄕㄤ
    (C) ㄧ ㄐㄧㄥ
    (D) ㄌㄧ ㄎㄜ

47. Wǒ ___ qù guò tú shū guǎn le.
    (A) xiǎng yào
    (B) mǎ shàng
    (C) yǐ jīng
    (D) lì kè

48. 我們打算去打球的，___ 因為下雨，所以沒去。

   (A) 原來
   (B) 後來
   (C) 本來
   (D) 才來

48. 我们打算去打球的，___ 因为下雨，所以没去。

   (A) 原来
   (B) 后来
   (C) 本来
   (D) 才来

48. ㄨㄛˇ ㄇㄣ˙ ㄉㄚˇ ㄙㄨㄢˋ ㄑㄩˋ ㄉㄚˇ ㄑㄧㄡˊ ㄉㄜ˙，___ ㄧㄣ ㄨㄟˋ ㄒㄧㄚˋ ㄩˇ，ㄙㄨㄛˇ ㄧˇ ㄇㄟˊ ㄑㄩˋ。

   (A) ㄩㄢˊ ㄌㄞˊ
   (B) ㄏㄡˋ ㄌㄞˊ
   (C) ㄅㄣˇ ㄌㄞˊ
   (D) ㄘㄞˊ ㄌㄞˊ

48. Wǒ men dǎ suàn qù dǎ qiú de, ___ yīn wèi xià yǔ, suǒ yǐ méi qù.

   (A) yuán lái
   (B) hòu lái
   (C) běn lái
   (D) cái lái

---

49. 「守株待兔」是一句中國的___。

   (A) 詩詞
   (B) 小說
   (C) 名言
   (D) 成語

49. 「守株待兔」是一句中国的___。

   (A) 诗词
   (B) 小说
   (C) 名言
   (D) 成语

49. 「ㄕㄡˇ ㄓㄨ ㄉㄞˋ ㄊㄨˋ」ㄕˋ ㄧˊ ㄐㄩˋ ㄓㄨㄥ ㄍㄨㄛˊ ㄉㄜ˙ ___。

   (A) ㄕ ㄘˊ
   (B) ㄒㄧㄠˇ ㄕㄨㄛ
   (C) ㄇㄧㄥˊ ㄧㄢˊ
   (D) ㄔㄥˊ ㄩˇ

49. "Shǒu zhū dài tù" shì yí jù Zhōngguó de ___ .

   (A) shī cí
   (B) xiǎo shuō
   (C) míng yán
   (D) chéng yǔ

---

50. ___ 不喜歡，___ 買回來呢？

   (A) 雖然…可是
   (B) 既然…又何必
   (C) 因為…所以
   (D) 除了…為什麼

50. ___ 不喜欢，___ 买回来呢？

   (A) 虽然…可是
   (B) 既然…又何必
   (C) 因为…所以
   (D) 除了…为什么

50. ___ ㄅㄨˋ ㄒㄧˇ ㄏㄨㄢ，___ ㄇㄞˇ ㄏㄨㄟˊ ㄌㄞˊ ㄋㄜ˙？

   (A) ㄙㄨㄟ ㄖㄢˊ…ㄎㄜˇ ㄕˋ
   (B) ㄐㄧˋ ㄖㄢˊ…ㄧㄡˋ ㄏㄜˊ ㄅㄧˋ
   (C) ㄧㄣ ㄨㄟˋ…ㄙㄨㄛˇ ㄧˇ
   (D) ㄔㄨˊ ㄌㄜ˙…ㄨㄟˋ ㄕㄣˊ ㄇㄜ˙

50. ___ bù xǐ huān, ___ mǎi huí lái ne?

   (A) Suī rán .... kě shì
   (B) Jì rán .... yòu hé bì
   (C) Yīn wèi .... suǒ yǐ
   (D) Chú le .... wèi shén me

51. 小姐，請問寄___中國的信，郵費是六毛錢嗎？
   (A) 在
   (B) 來
   (C) 成
   (D) 到

51. ㄒㄧㄠˇㄐㄧㄝˇ，ㄑㄧㄥˇㄨㄣˋㄐㄧˋ___ㄓㄨㄥㄍㄨㄛˊㄉㄜˉㄒㄧㄣˋ，ㄧㄡˊㄈㄟˋㄕˋㄌㄧㄡˋㄇㄠˊㄑㄧㄢˊㄇㄚ˙？
   (A) ㄗㄞˋ
   (B) ㄌㄞˊ
   (C) ㄔㄥˊ
   (D) ㄉㄠˋ

51. 小姐，请问寄___中国的信，邮费是六毛钱吗？
   (A) 在
   (B) 来
   (C) 成
   (D) 到

51. Xiǎo jiě, qǐng wèn jì ___ Zhōngguó de xìn, yóu fèi shì liù máo qián ma?
   (A) zài
   (B) lái
   (C) chéng
   (D) dào

---

52. ___你一直幫他做作業，___害了他。
   (A) 既然 … 於是
   (B) 雖然 … 可是
   (C) 除了 … 還是
   (D) 如果 … 反而

52. ___ㄋㄧˇㄧˋㄓˊㄅㄤㄊㄚㄗㄨㄛˋㄗㄨㄛˋㄧㄝˋ，___ㄏㄞˋㄌㄜ˙ㄊㄚ。
   (A) ㄐㄧˋㄖㄢˊ … ㄩˊㄕˋ
   (B) ㄙㄨㄟㄖㄢˊ … ㄎㄜˇㄕˋ
   (C) ㄔㄨˊㄌㄜ˙ … ㄏㄞˊㄕˋ
   (D) ㄖㄨˊㄍㄨㄛˇ … ㄈㄢˇㄦˊ

52. ___你一直帮他做作业，___害了他。
   (A) 既然 … 於是
   (B) 虽然 … 可是
   (C) 除了 … 还是
   (D) 如果 … 反而

52. ___ nǐ yì zhí bāng tā zuò zuò yè, ___hài le tā.
   (A) Jì rán .... yú shì
   (B) Suī rán .... kě shì
   (C) Chú le .... hái shì
   (D) Rú guǒ .... fǎn ér

---

53. 他___家裏有急事，___請了一天假。
   (A) 因此 … 所以
   (B) 因而 … 可是
   (C) 原因 … 只有
   (D) 因爲 … 所以

53. ㄊㄚ___ㄐㄧㄚㄌㄧˇㄧㄡˇㄐㄧˊㄕˋ，___ㄑㄧㄥˇㄌㄜ˙ㄧˋㄊㄧㄢㄐㄧㄚˋ。
   (A) ㄧㄣ ㄘˇ … ㄙㄨㄛˇㄧˇ
   (B) ㄧㄣ ㄦˊ … ㄎㄜˇㄕˋ
   (C) ㄩㄢˊㄧㄣ … ㄓˇㄧㄡˇ
   (D) ㄧㄣ ㄨㄟˋ … ㄙㄨㄛˇㄧˇ

53. 他___家里有急事，___请了一天假。
   (A) 因此 … 所以
   (B) 因而 … 可是
   (C) 原因 … 只有
   (D) 因为 … 所以

53. Tā ___ jiā lǐ yǒu jí shì, ___ qǐng le yì tiān jià.
   (A) yīn cǐ .... suǒ yǐ
   (B) yīn ér .... kě shì
   (C) yuán yīn .... zhǐ yǒu
   (D) yīn wèi .... suǒ yǐ

54. 我們在購物中心逛了很久，___買了一些想要的東西。

(A) 於是
(B) 因爲
(C) 終於
(D) 原來

54. 我们在购物中心逛了很久，___买了一些想要的东西。

(A) 於是
(B) 因为
(C) 终於
(D) 原来

54. ㄨㄛˇ ㄇㄣ˙ ㄗㄞˋ ㄍㄡˋ ㄨˋ ㄓㄨㄥ ㄒㄧㄣ ㄍㄨㄤˋ ㄌㄜ˙ ㄏㄣˇ ㄐㄧㄡˇ ，___ ㄇㄞˇ ㄌㄜ˙ ㄧˋ ㄒㄧㄝ ㄒㄧㄤˇ ㄧㄠˋ ㄉㄜ˙ ㄉㄨㄥ ㄒㄧ˙ 。

(A) ㄩˊ ㄕˋ
(B) ㄧㄣ ㄨㄟˋ
(C) ㄓㄨㄥ ㄩˊ
(D) ㄩㄢˊ ㄌㄞˊ

54. Wǒ men zài gòu wù zhōng xīn guàng le hěn jiǔ, ___ mǎi le yì xiē xiǎng yào de dōng xi.

(A) yú shì
(B) yīn wèi
(C) zhōng yú
(D) yuán lái

---

55. 他在武術學校裏學會了拳打腳踢，讓我們 ____ 吃驚。

(A) 十分
(B) 一起
(C) 一直
(D) 一會兒

55. 他在武术学校里学会了拳打脚踢，让我们 ____ 吃惊。

(A) 十分
(B) 一起
(C) 一直
(D) 一会儿

55. ㄊㄚ ㄗㄞˋ ㄨˇ ㄕㄨˋ ㄒㄩㄝˊ ㄒㄧㄠˋ ㄌㄧˇ ㄒㄩㄝˊ ㄏㄨㄟˋ ㄌㄜ˙ ㄑㄩㄢˊ ㄉㄚˇ ㄐㄧㄠˇ ㄊㄧ ，ㄖㄤˋ ㄨㄛˇ ㄇㄣ˙ ____ ㄔ ㄐㄧㄥ 。

(A) ㄕˊ ㄈㄣ
(B) ㄧˋ ㄑㄧˇ
(C) ㄧˋ ㄓˊ
(D) ㄧˋ ㄏㄨㄟˇ ㄦ

55. Tā zài wǔ shù xué xiào lǐ xué huì le quán dǎ jiǎo tī, ràng wǒ men ____ chī jīng.

(A) shí fēn
(B) yì qǐ
(C) yì zhí
(D) yì huǐr

SAT II 中文模擬試題 第一套
Section III : Reading Comprehension

Directions: Read the following selections carefully for comprehension. Each selection is followed by one or more questions or incomplete statements based on its content. Select the answer or completion that is best according to the passage and fill in the corresponding oval on the answer sheet.

THIS SECTION OF THE TEST IS PRESENTED IN TWO WRITING SYSTEMS: TRADITIONAL CHARACTERS AND SIMPLIFIED CHARACTERS. IT IS RECOMMENDED THAT YOU CHOOSE ONLY THAT WRITING SYSTEM WITH WHICH YOU ARE MOST FAMILIAR AS YOU WORK THROUGH THIS SECTION OF THE TEST.

56~57

中國明日主要城市氣象預報

城市	天氣	最低氣溫	最高氣溫
北京	晴轉陰	-9	1
上海	小雨	11	14
西安	小雪轉陰	-5	3
拉薩	多雲	-6	11

中国明日主要城市气象预报

城市	天气	最低气温	最高气温
北京	晴转阴	-9	1
上海	小雨	11	14
西安	小雪转阴	-5	3
拉萨	多云	-6	11

Question 56 How is Xi'an's weather going to be tomorrow?

(A) mostly cloudy

(B) light rain

(C) light snow, then cloudy

(D) sunny, then cloudy

Question 57 What will be the lowest temperature of Beijing?

(A) 1

(B) -9

(C) 3

(D) -5

58~59

泡茶方法：

　　要飲好茶，首先要將小茶壺以開水燙熱，然後放進三分之一茶葉，注入開水。第一次沖泡的茶，含鹼澀味，應立即倒掉。第二次沖泡的茶，便可開始飲用。

泡茶方法：

　　要饮好茶，首先要将小茶壶以开水烫热，然后放进三分之一茶叶，注入开水。第一次冲泡的茶，含硷涩味，应立即倒掉。第二次冲泡的茶，便可开始饮用。

Question 58　　What kind of water is used to make tea?

　　(A)　hot water

　　(B)　warm water

　　(C)　ice water

　　(D)　boiling water

Question 59　　When is the best moment to drink the tea?

　　(A)　when the tea is infused for the first time

　　(B)　when the tea is infused for the second time

　　(C)　wait until the tea is cool

　　(D)　when you are thirsty

60

全球日報

　電話總機　*223-408-3678*（10線）

　訂報專線　*1-800-888-7957*

　分類廣告　*1-800-888-1388*

　傳真號碼　*223-408-8763*

全球日报

　电话总机　*223-408-3678*（10线）

　订报专线　*1-800-888-7957*

　分类广告　*1-800-888-1388*

　传真号码　*223-408-8763*

Question 60　　Which number is the fax number?

　　(A)　223-408-3678

　　(B)　1-800-888-7957

　　(C)　1-800-888-1388

　　(D)　223-408-8763

61

哈林遊樂場	哈林遊乐场
聖誕節大酬賓	***圣诞节大酬宾***
◆ 來回巴士團 $20（兩人同行，一人半價）	◆ 来回巴士团 $20（两人同行，一人半价）
◆ 過夜巴士團 $35	◆ 过夜巴士团 $35
◆ 飛機團　　　$25	◆ 飞机团　　　$25
◆ 自助開車團 $10	◆ 自助开车团 $10

Question 61　　How much does the overnight bus option cost?

    (A)　$ 20

    (B)　$ 35

    (C)　$ 25

    (D)　$ 10

62~63

♥ 愛心健康講座	♥ 愛心健康讲座
時間：十月九日(六) 10:00am-11:30am	时间：十月九日(六) 10:00am-11:30am
講師：心臟內科 李明亮醫師	讲师：心脏内科 李明亮医师
內容：如何預防心臟病的發生	内容：如何预防心脏病的发生
地點：愛心醫院大禮堂	地点：爱心医院大礼堂

Question 62　　Where is the location of the speech?

    (A)　cafeteria

    (B)　auditorium

    (C)　church

    (D)　conference room

Question 63　　What is the topic of the speech?

    (A)　how to prevent heart disease

    (B)　how to take care of heart patients

    (C)　love stories

    (D)　how to help other people

小華：

　　我和姑媽先去購物中心買份送爺爺的生日禮物，然後再去餐館。你在家先把西裝換好，並配條領帶。等爸爸下班回來接你，我們六點半在那邊碰面。

媽媽

小华：

　　我和姑妈先去购物中心买份送爷爷的生日礼物，然后再去餐馆。你在家先把西装换好，并配条领带。等爸爸下班回来接你，我们六点半在那边碰面。

妈妈

Question 64　　Where are they going to meet?

(A) at a restaurant

(B) at a shopping mall

(C) at aunt's house

(D) at grandpa's house

Question 65　　Who went with Mom to buy a present?

(A) father

(B) grandpa

(C) mother's sister

(D) father's sister

Question 66　　To whom is the note addressed?

(A) father

(B) son

(C) daughter

(D) aunt

Question 67　　Why are they buying a present?

(A) grandpa's birthday

(B) parent's anniversary

(C) Christmas

(D) aunt's birthday

大頭：

　　今天的歷史考試難不難？我可能昨晚吃壞了，一直在拉肚子，今天睡了一天。你知不知道數學老師的網址，請用電子郵件寄給我好嗎？我想看看有什麼作業。謝謝！

安力

大头：

　　今天的历史考试难不难？我可能昨晚吃坏了，一直在拉肚子，今天睡了一天。你知不知道数学老师的网址，请用电子邮件寄给我好吗？我想看看有什么作业。谢谢！

安力

Question 68　　Why was the writer absent from school?

(A)　　ate too much last night

(B)　　diarrhea

(C)　　had a cold

(D)　　overslept

Question 69　　What test did the writer miss?

(A)　　history test

(B)　　math test

(C)　　computer test

(D)　　reading test

Question 70　　What did the writer ask his friend to send to him?

(A)　　math homework

(B)　　history review

(C)　　the math teacher's web site

(D)　　note for sick leave

 # 71~72

最新消息！史無前例！

北京市近日連續開設三家
民辦古典藝術博物館

最新消息！史无前例！

北京市近日连续开设三家
民办古典艺术博物馆

Question 71 The news is about

(A) a classical art museum

(B) an art gallery

(C) an antique shop

(D) a library

Question 72 Which of the following is correct?

(A) They are owned by the government.

(B) They are owned by the city of Beijing.

(C) They are owned by private companies.

(D) It is a co-operative museum owned by three private companies.

 # 73~74

學校今年舉辦辯論比賽，一共有五
隊報名參加。本班也派出六位同學
組隊參加，四位女生，兩位男生。
經過三個小時的比賽，本班獲得了
亞軍。

学校今年举办辩论比赛，一共有五
队报名参加。本班也派出六位同学
组队参加，四位女生，两位男生。
经过三个小时的比赛，本班获得了
亚军。

Question 73 How many teams entered the meet?

(A) 6 teams

(B) 5 teams

(C) 4 teams

(D) 3 teams

Question 74   How did the author's team do?

(A)   They won first place.

(B)   They won second place.

(C)   They won third place.

(D)   They won fourth place.

 # 75~76

親愛的林老師： 　　今天早上我們到學校上課時，沒見到您，都覺得非常奇怪。後來校長來告訴我們，說您生病，進了醫院，請陳老師代課。我們聽了都很難過。 　　我們在學校裏，一切都好，請您安心休養，不要掛念。敬祝 　　早日康復 　　　　　　學生 王大中 敬上	亲爱的林老师： 　　今天早上我们到学校上课时，没见到您，都觉得非常奇怪。后来校长来告诉我们，说您生病，进了医院，请陈老师代课。我们听了都很难过。 　　我们在学校里，一切都好，请您安心休养，不要挂念。敬祝 　　早日康复 　　　　　　学生 王大中 敬上

Question 75   The letter tells us that

(A)   Lin is a teacher and Wang is a student.

(B)   Lin is the principal and Chen is a teacher.

(C)   Wang and Chen are both students.

(D)   Lin and Wang are both students.

Question 76   Who called in sick?

(A)   Wang

(B)   Chen

(C)   the principal

(D)   Lin

77

護照遺失
本人林振標遺失中華
人民共和國護照一本
號碼 No. 858613 特此
聲明作廢

護照遺失
本人林振标遗失中华
人民共和国护照一本
号码 No. 858613 特此
声明作废

Question 77   What is this ad for?

(A)   an official notice

(B)   a news statement

(C)   a missing passport announcement

(D)   a business agreement

78

電子廠急徵
急徵各類電子板裝配員十數名、測
試技術員及司機各一名，需具英語
聽講能力。請於每日下午2：30後，
至 41441 S. Grimmer Blvd, Fremont 面試

電子厂急徵
急徵各类电子板装配员十数名、测
试技术员及司机各一名，需具英语
听讲能力。请於每日下午2：30后，
至 41441 S. Grimmer Blvd, Fremont 面试

Question 78   What is the basic requirement for all applicants?

(A)   to have a driver's license

(B)   to have technical skills

(C)   to have the ability to speak English

(D)   to have electronics background

79

三星牙科中心
朱柏松牙醫博士
（408）259-5660
各種牙科治療
成人、兒童牙齒矯正

三星牙科中心
朱柏松牙医博士
（408）259-5660
各种牙科治疗
成人、儿童牙齿矫正

Question 79   What is this advertisement about?

(A)   shopping center

(B)   dental service

(C)   school information

(D)   bus station

80~81

彩虹彩色沖印公司
價格：沖洗整卷每張四角
　　　加洗單張五角五分
時間：隔天可取
地點：格林大道88號

彩虹彩色沖印公司
价格：沖洗整卷每張四角
　　　加洗单张五角五分
时间：隔天可取
地点：格林大道88号

Question 80   The cost of reprinting one picture is

(A) $ 0.55

(B) $ 0.40

(C)   free of charge

(D) $ 0.88

Question 81   When will the pictures be ready?

(A)   the next day

(B)   in two days

(C)   in three days

(D)   next week

 # 82

教授鋼琴

著名音樂學院鋼琴碩士，加州音樂
教師協會會員，教授各種程度學生
，多年經驗，可到府上授課

408-227-4151

教授钢琴

著名音乐学院钢琴硕士，加州音乐
教师协会会员，教授各种程度学生
，多年经验，可到府上授课

408-227-4151

Question 82 Who placed the advertisement?

    (A)   a piano student

    (B)   a violin student

    (C)   a piano teacher

    (D)   a violin teacher

 # 83~84

佳樂美容院

農曆新年八折優待

男女髮型設計、洗、剪、吹

佳乐美容院

农历新年八折优待

男女发型设计、洗、剪、吹

Question 83 This is a

    (A)   marriage announcement

    (B)   personal ad

    (C)   clothing ad

    (D)   hair salon ad

Question 84 What is the advertised discount?

    (A)   20% off

    (B)   40% off

    (C)   60% off

    (D)   80% off

85

二　月

星期日	星期一	星期二	星期三	星期四	星期五	星期六
					1 十二月廿	2 廿一
3 廿二	4 立春	5 廿四	6 廿五	7 廿六	8 廿七	9 廿八
10 廿九	11 三十	12 正月	13 初二	14 初三	15 初四	16 初五
17 初六	18 初七	19 初八	20 初九	21 初十	22 十一	23 十二
24 十三	25 十四	26 十五	27 十六	28 十七		

二　月

星期日	星期一	星期二	星期三	星期四	星期五	星期六
					1 十二月廿	2 廿一
3 廿二	4 立春	5 廿四	6 廿五	7 廿六	8 廿七	9 廿八
10 廿九	11 三十	12 正月	13 初二	14 初三	15 初四	16 初五
17 初六	18 初七	19 初八	20 初九	21 初十	22 十一	23 十二
24 十三	25 十四	26 十五	27 十六	28 十七		

Question 85　　When is the lunar New Year's day?

(A)　February 1

(B)　February 4

(C)　February 12

(D)　January 1

SAT II 中文模擬試卷 第二套
Section I : Listening Comprehension

Part A

Directions: In this part of the test you will hear short questions, statements, or exchanges in Mandarin Chinese, follow by three responses designated (A), (B), and (C). You will hear the statements or questions, as well as the responses, just one time and they are not printed in your test booklet. Therefore, you must listen very carefully. Select the best response and fill in the corresponding oval on your answer sheet. You will have 15 seconds to answer each question.

Question 1   (A)   (B)   (C)

Question 2   (A)   (B)   (C)

Question 3   (A)   (B)   (C)

Question 4   (A)   (B)   (C)

Question 5   (A)   (B)   (C)

Question 6   (A)   (B)   (C)

Question 7   (A)   (B)   (C)

Question 8   (A)   (B)   (C)

Question 9   (A)   (B)   (C)

Question 10   (A)   (B)   (C)

Question 11   (A)   (B)   (C)

Question 12   (A)   (B)   (C)

Question 13   (A)   (B)   (C)

Question 14   (A)   (B)   (C)

Question 15   (A)   (B)   (C)

Part B

Directions: You will now hear a series of short selections. You will hear them only once and they are not printed in your test booklet. After each selection, you will be asked one or more questions about what you have just heard. These questions, with four possible answers, are printed in your test booklet. Select the best answer to each question from among the four choices given and fill in the corresponding oval on your answer sheet. You will have 15 seconds to answer each question.

 # 16~17

Question 16   Why did the man call?

(A)   to return a call

(B)   to ask her out

(C)   to tell her Spanish class was rescheduled

(D)   to ask her what the Spanish homework was

Question 17   Why didn't the woman pick up the phone earlier?

(A)   She wasn't at home.

(B)   She was at Spanish class.

(C)   She was in the bathroom.

(D)   She was asleep.

 # 18

Question 18   What is wrong with the woman's teeth?

(A)   She has a loose tooth.

(B)   She has a chipped tooth.

(C)   Her braces are too tight.

(D)   She has a big cavity.

 # 19~20

Question 19   Why might she not come home during winter vacation?

(A)   She might go on vacation.

(B)   She might need to work on her experiment.

(C)   Plane tickets are too expensive.

(D)   She might visit her friends.

Question 20   What did her father say?

    (A)   take care of yourself

    (B)   study hard

    (C)   work hard on your experiment

    (D)   remember to call home

21~22

Question 21   Mr. Wang is

    (A)   a professor

    (B)   a writer

    (C)   a lawyer

    (D)   a reporter

Question 22   Why do they want Mr. Wong to treat them?

    (A)   because he got a check from the newspaper office

    (B)   because he got a pay raise

    (C)   because he won the lottery

    (D)   because he found a job with the newspaper office

23

Question 23   What is the $50 for?

    (A)   rebate for installing a water-saving toilet

    (B)   to pay the water bill

    (C)   to replace their faucets

    (D)   rebate for installing new sinks

24

Question 24   What type of film did they watch today?

    (A)   a romantic film

    (B)   an animated film

    (C)   a detective film

    (D)   a science-fiction film

25~26

Question 25   What services does the man want from the photo shop?

(A)   film developing and reprints

(B)   film developing and buy a roll of new film

(C)   film developing and enlargements

(D)   reprints and enlargements

Question 26   Why does the photo shop clerk say that they have good services?

(A)   The store open at 9:30 am every day.

(B)   They charge at very low price for film developing.

(C)   They don't charge for film developing if customers are not satisfied with the results.

(D)   If you drop off the film before 9:30 am, you can pick it up at 3:00 pm the next day.

27~28

Question 27   Which of the following statements is true about the apartment rental?

(A)   no furniture will be provided

(B)   rent does not include utility bills

(C)   no pets allowed

(D)   has two parking spaces

Question 28   What is the marital status of the person asking about the apartment rental?

(A)   a single man

(B)   married without kids

(C)   not mentioned

(D)   married with kid(s)

 # 29

Question 29   In which way did the man decide to mail his package?

        (A)   by express

        (B)   by surface mail plus registered

        (C)   by air mail

        (D)   by air mail plus registered

 # 30

Question 30   Why did the child not do well on his math test?

        (A)   He mistook addition problems with subtraction.

        (B)   He wrote too slow.

        (C)   He mistook multiplication problems for division.

        (D)   There were too many problems to solve in the test.

SAT II 中文模擬試題 第二套
Section I : Listening Comprehension

Part A

Directions: In this part of the test you will hear short questions, statements, or exchanges in Mandarin Chinese, followed by three responses designated (A), (B), and (C). You will hear the statements or questions, as well as the responses, just one time and they are not printed in your test booklet. Therefore, you must listen very carefully. Select the best response and fill in the corresponding oval on your answer sheet. You will have 15 seconds to answer each question.

Question 1

A：小王，你學過電腦嗎？

B：只是皮毛而已，還請你多多指教。

   (A) 小王的電腦非常好。

   (B) 小王才懂一點點電腦。

   (C) 小王在教電腦。

Question 2

我覺得你很面熟，我們在哪兒見過嗎？

   (A) 好久不見，你好嗎？

   (B) 你忘了，上次在王伯伯家一起吃過飯。

   (C) 我覺得麵沒煮熟。

Question 3

真後悔沒聽媽媽的話，淋了個落湯雞。

   (A) 媽媽燒了一鍋雞湯。

   (B) 媽媽把醬汁淋在雞肉上。

   (C) 看！我全身都濕了。

Question 4

你搬來不久,地方還不太熟吧!

    (A) 是呀!我只知道住家附近的路。

    (B) 這些菜煮得太熟了。

    (C) 我和班上的同學不熟。

Question 5

他家的電話一直打不通。

    (A) 他一定又在上網了。

    (B) 太晚了,不方便打電話。

    (C) 我不知道他家的電話號碼。

Question 6

李小明在電話裏說,他十點左右會過來。

    (A) 他可能會從右邊那條街走來。

    (B) 九點五十五分了,他應該快到了。

    (C) 他十一點以後才會來。

Question 7

他找房子找了兩個星期,你知道有誰要出租房子?

    (A) 好像張太太正在找房客。

    (B) 他想找間可以度假兩個星期的房子。

    (C) 他搬到這間房子兩個星期了。

Question 8

A:王經理,最近公司的生意怎麼樣?

B:托您的福,還馬馬虎虎。

    (A) 公司的生意還過得去。

    (B) 你做事馬馬虎虎,怎麼開公司?

    (C) 我的朋友想和你們公司做生意。

Question 9

你真不簡單，才到中國三年，中文就說得這麼道地。

    (A) 我只會說很簡單的中文。

    (B) 我的中國朋友教我，所以我才能學這麼快。

    (C) 我不怎麼會說中文。

Question 10

A：明天的考試，你準備好了嗎？

B：差不多，只是我怕早上起不來，怎麼辦？

    (A) 我的功課很差。

    (B) 早點睡，記得用鬧鐘。

    (C) 考試的時候寫快一點。

Question 11

到現在，我們還沒辦法正確地預測什麼時候會發生地震，所以才會這麼可怕！

    (A) 昨天發生六級的地震。

    (B) 我們還不能知道哪一天會有地震。

    (C) 地震搖得太厲害了，我們沒辦法站穩。

Question 12

A：你總共有幾件行李？

B：兩件托運，一件隨身攜帶。

    (A) 行李太大，我幫你拖。

    (B) 有兩件行李還沒有運到。

    (C) 手提行李一件。

Question 13

這次露營玩得真痛快！頭兩天都是三更半夜才去睡！

    (A) 昨晚玩到很晚才睡，所以頭很痛。

    (B) 這次露營玩得好愉快！

    (C) 夜深了，地上有很多露水。

Question 14

這次失敗了，不要灰心，我相信你一定可以克服所有的困難。

    (A) 我對你有信心，你一定會成功。

    (B) 我相信你會喜歡這件灰色的夾克。

    (C) 碰到困難，記得寫信給我。

Question 15

現在海關都會很仔細地檢查護照，甚至也會抽查旅客的鞋子。

    (A) 謝謝你的關心，護士已經幫我檢查過了。

    (B) 現在海關對搭機的旅客，檢查特別小心。

    (C) 出外旅行前，一定要檢查家裏的門窗有沒有關好。

Part B

Directions: You will now hear a series of short selections. You will hear them <u>only once</u> and they are not printed in your test booklet. After each selection, you will be asked one or more questions about what you have just heard. These questions, with four possible answers, are printed in your test booklet. Select the best answer to each question from among the four choices given and fill in the corresponding oval on your answer sheet. You will have 15 seconds to answer each question.

Question 16~17

男：喂！小美嗎？我剛才打了兩通電話都沒人接。

女：對不起！我剛才在浴室，沒聽到鈴聲。

男：我要告訴你，明天的西班牙文上課時間改到下午三點。

女：謝謝你通知我。

Question 18

女：王醫生，我的牙齒很痛，吃止痛藥都沒有用。

男：哇！你有一顆牙蛀了個大洞，可能需要拔掉。

Question 19~20

女：爸爸，時候不早了，我該登機了。

男：出門在外，要好好照顧自己。

女：寒假要做實驗，如果抽得出一個星期的空檔，我會回來；否則明年暑假一定會回來。

Question 21~22

女：王先生，你上個月投的那篇文章，有沒有消息？

男：文章被登出來了，我剛剛收到報社寄來的支票。

女：領了稿費，該請客了。

Question 23

女：今年夏天缺水，加州水公司提醒大家節約用水。

男：聽說如果每換裝一個省水馬桶，可以退款五十元。

女：那我們家三間洗手間的馬桶趕快換吧！

Question 24

男：你喜歡今天這部電影嗎？

女：這部偵探片太刺激了，把我嚇出了一身冷汗。

男：你真是個電影迷，不管什麼文藝片、喜劇片、卡通片、科幻片，你都喜歡看。

Question 25~26

男：我有一卷底片要洗，另外兩張照片要放大，什麼時候可以來拿？

女：我們店裏服務特別好，只要早上九點半以前送來，保證明天下午三點就可以拿到，否則免費。

男：真的，那兩張放大的，明天也可以一起拿嗎？

女：放大的需要一個星期。

Question 27~28

男：請問還有公寓要出租嗎？

女：有啊！一房一廳，附帶傢俱和一個停車位。

男：聽起來很適合像我這樣的單身漢。每個月租金多少？

女：五百塊，押金一個月，包括水電，不過不准養寵物。

Question 29

男：這個包裹很重要，我想要寄掛號的。

女：沒問題，要用海運還是空運，兩種運費差三十塊。海運約需一個半月，空運一個星期。如果用快遞只需兩天，但是運費貴多了。

男：沒那麼急，下星期六能收到就好了。

女：運費是四十二塊。

Question 30

男：媽媽，我這次數學考得不好。

女：怎麼這麼粗心，好多題目，你都把乘法看成除法。

男：我下次會小心一點。

女：平常要多練習，速度就會加快。

Section II : Grammar

Directions: This section consists of a number of incomplete statements, each of which has four suggested completions. Select the word or phrase that best completes the sentence structurally and logically. Please fill in the corresponding oval on the answer sheet.

THE QUESTIONS ARE PRESENTED IN FOUR DIFFERENT WRITING SYSTEMS: TRADITIONAL CHARACTERS, SIMPLIFIED CHARACTERS, PINYIN ROMANIZATION, AND CHINESE PHONETIC ALPHABET(BO PO MO FO). TO SAVE TIME, IT IS RECOMMENDED THAT YOU CHOOSE THE WRITING SYSTEM WITH WHICH YOU ARE MOST FAMILIAR WITH AND **READ ONLY THAT VERSION OF THE QUESTION.**

31. 你去超級市場的時候＿＿幫我買一包麵粉。

    (A) 方便
    (B) 便宜
    (C) 便利
    (D) 順便

31. 你去超级市场的时候＿＿帮我买一包面粉。

    (A) 方便
    (B) 便宜
    (C) 便利
    (D) 顺便

31. ㄋㄧˇ ㄑㄩˋ ㄔㄠ ㄐㄧˊ ㄕˋ ㄔㄤˇ ㄉㄜ˙ ㄕˊ ㄏㄡˋ ＿＿ ㄅㄤ ㄨㄛˇ ㄇㄞˇ ㄧˋ ㄅㄠ ㄇㄧㄢˋ ㄈㄣˇ。

    (A) ㄈㄤ ㄅㄧㄢˋ
    (B) ㄆㄧㄢˊ ㄧ
    (C) ㄅㄧㄢˋ ㄌㄧˋ
    (D) ㄕㄨㄣˋ ㄅㄧㄢˋ

31. Nǐ qù chāo jí shì chǎng de shí hòu ＿＿bāng wǒ mǎi yì bāo miàn fěn.

    (A) fāng biàn
    (B) pián yí
    (C) biàn lì
    (D) shùn biàn

32. 他＿＿＿＿地跑出去，不知道發生什麼事？

    (A) 急急忙忙
    (B) 高高低低
    (C) 安安靜靜
    (D) 仔仔細細

32. 他＿＿＿＿地跑出去，不知道发生什么事？

    (A) 急急忙忙
    (B) 高高低低
    (C) 安安静静
    (D) 仔仔细细

32. ㄊㄚ ＿＿＿＿ ㄉㄜ˙ ㄆㄠˇ ㄔㄨ ㄑㄩˋ，ㄅㄨˋ ㄓ ㄉㄠˋ ㄈㄚ ㄕㄥ ㄕㄣˊ ㄕˋ？

    (A) ㄐㄧˊ ㄐㄧˊ ㄇㄤˊ ㄇㄤˊ
    (B) ㄍㄠ ㄍㄠ ㄉㄧ ㄉㄧ
    (C) ㄢ ㄢ ㄐㄧㄥˋ ㄐㄧㄥˋ
    (D) ㄗˇ ㄗˇ ㄒㄧˋ ㄒㄧˋ

32. Tā ＿＿＿＿ de pǎo chū qù, bù zhī dào fā shēng shén me shì?

    (A) jí jí máng máng
    (B) gāo gāo dī dī
    (C) ān ān jìng jìng
    (D) zǐ zǐ xì xì

33. ＿＿外面下著大雨，我＿＿要出門。

    (A) 當然…還有

    (B) 雖然…還是

    (C) 不然…還沒

    (D) 忽然…還能

33. ＿＿外面下著大雨，我＿＿要出门。

    (A) 当然…还有

    (B) 虽然…还是

    (C) 不然…还没

    (D) 忽然…还能

33. ＿＿ㄨㄞˋ ㄇㄧㄢˋ ㄒㄧㄚˋ ㄓㄜ˙ ㄉㄚˋ ㄩˇ，ㄨㄛˇ ＿＿ㄧㄠˋ ㄔㄨ ㄇㄣˊ。

    (A) ㄉㄤ ㄖㄢˊ … ㄏㄞˊ ㄧㄡˇ

    (B) ㄙㄨㄟ ㄖㄢˊ … ㄏㄞˊ ㄕˋ

    (C) ㄅㄨˋ ㄖㄢˊ … ㄏㄞˊ ㄇㄟˊ

    (D) ㄏㄨ ㄖㄢˊ … ㄏㄞˊ ㄋㄥˊ

33. ＿＿wài miàn xià zhe dà yǔ, wǒ＿＿yào chū mén.

    (A) Dāng rán .... hái yǒu

    (B) Suī rán .... hái shì

    (C) Bù rán .... hái méi

    (D) Hū rán .... hái néng

34. ＿＿＿有什麼事，就打電話給我。

    (A) 千萬

    (B) 一萬

    (C) 萬萬

    (D) 萬一

34. ＿＿＿有什么事，就打电话给我。

    (A) 千万

    (B) 一万

    (C) 万万

    (D) 万一

34. ＿＿＿ㄧㄡˇ ㄕㄣˊ ㄇㄜ˙ ㄕˋ，ㄐㄧㄡˋ ㄉㄚˇ ㄉㄧㄢˋ ㄏㄨㄚˋ ㄍㄟˇ ㄨㄛˇ。

    (A) ㄑㄧㄢ ㄨㄢˋ

    (B) ㄧˊ ㄨㄢˋ

    (C) ㄨㄢˋ ㄨㄢˋ

    (D) ㄨㄢˋ ㄧ

34. ＿＿＿ yǒu shén me shì, jiù dǎ diàn huà gěi wǒ.

    (A) Qiān wàn

    (B) Yí wàn

    (C) Wàn wàn

    (D) Wàn yī

35. ＿＿ 我＿＿洗澡的時候，電話鈴響了。

    (A) 是 … 正當

    (B) 當 … 正在

    (C) 正在 … 是

    (D) 除了 … 以外

35. ＿＿ 我＿＿洗澡的时候，电话铃响了。

    (A) 是 … 正当

    (B) 当 … 正在

    (C) 正在 … 是

    (D) 除了 … 以外

35. ＿＿ ㄨㄛˇ ＿＿ ㄒㄧˇ ㄗㄠˇ ㄉㄜ˙ ㄕˊ ㄏㄡˋ，ㄉㄧㄢˋ ㄏㄨㄚˋ ㄌㄧㄥˊ ㄒㄧㄤˇ ㄌㄜ˙。

    (A) ㄕˋ … ㄓㄥˋ ㄉㄤ

    (B) ㄉㄤ … ㄓㄥˋ ㄗㄞˋ

    (C) ㄓㄥˋ ㄗㄞˋ … ㄕˋ

    (D) ㄔㄨˊ ㄌㄜ˙ … ㄧˇ ㄨㄞˋ

35. ＿＿ wǒ＿＿xǐ zǎo de shí hòu, diàn huà líng xiǎng le.

    (A) Shì.... zhèng dāng

    (B) Dāng .... zhèng zài

    (C) Zhèng zài .... shì

    (D) Chú le .... yǐ wài

36. ＿＿你说破了嘴，我 ＿＿不會答應。
    (A) 提起⋯就
    (B) 看⋯還
    (C) 就算⋯還是
    (D) 如果⋯會

36. ＿＿你说破了嘴，我 ＿＿不会答应。
    (A) 提起⋯就
    (B) 看⋯还
    (C) 就算⋯还是
    (D) 如果⋯会

36. ＿＿ nǐ shuō pò le zuǐ, wǒ ＿＿ bú huì dā yìng.
    (A) Tí qǐ .... jiù
    (B) Kàn .... hái
    (C) Jiù suàn .... hái shì
    (D) Rú guǒ .... huì

37. 哥哥的兒子＿＿＿＿的可愛極了。
    (A) 正正方方
    (B) 高高低低
    (C) 長長短短
    (D) 圓圓胖胖

37. 哥哥的儿子＿＿＿＿的可爱极了。
    (A) 正正方方
    (B) 高高低低
    (C) 长长短短
    (D) 圆圆胖胖

37. Gē ge de ér zi ＿＿＿＿ de kě ài jí le.
    (A) zhèng zhèng fāng fāng
    (B) gāo gāo dī dī
    (C) cháng cháng duǎn duǎn
    (D) yuán yuán pàng pàng

38. 這部電影真 ＿＿＿，我已經看過三遍了。
    (A) 不錯
    (B) 不好
    (C) 可以
    (D) 平凡

38. 这部电影真 ＿＿＿，我已经看过三遍了。
    (A) 不错
    (B) 不好
    (C) 可以
    (D) 平凡

38. Zhè bù diàn yǐng zhēn ＿＿＿, wǒ yǐ jīng kàn guò sān biàn le.
    (A) bú cuò
    (B) bù hǎo
    (C) kě yǐ
    (D) píng fán

39. 這次晚會 ___ 他負責。

   (A) 由

   (B) 從

   (C) 爲

   (D) 因

39. 这次晚会 ___ 他负责。

   (A) 由

   (B) 从

   (C) 为

   (D) 因

39. ㄓㄜˋ ㄘˋ ㄨㄢˇ ㄏㄨㄟˋ ___ ㄊㄚ ㄈㄨˋ ㄗㄜˊ 。

   (A) ㄧㄡˊ

   (B) ㄘㄨㄥˊ

   (C) ㄨㄟˋ

   (D) ㄧㄣ

39. Zhè cì wǎn huì ___ tā fù zé.

   (A) yóu

   (B) cóng

   (C) wèi

   (D) yīn

---

40. ___ 他說什麼，大家都不相信。

   (A) 無論

   (B) 總是

   (C) 除了

   (D) 雖然

40. ___ 他说什么，大家都不相信。

   (A) 无论

   (B) 总是

   (C) 除了

   (D) 虽然

40. ___ ㄊㄚ ㄕㄨㄛ ㄕㄣˊ ㄇㄜ˙ ，ㄉㄚˋ ㄐㄧㄚ ㄉㄡ ㄅㄨˋ ㄒㄧㄤ ㄒㄧㄣˋ 。

   (A) ㄨˊ ㄌㄨㄣˋ

   (B) ㄗㄨㄥˇ ㄕˋ

   (C) ㄔㄨˊ ㄌㄜ˙

   (D) ㄙㄨㄟ ㄖㄢˊ

40. ___ tā shuō shén me, dà jiā dōu bù xiāng xìn.

   (A) Wú lùn

   (B) Zǒng shì

   (C) Chú le

   (D) Suī rán

---

41. 現在壞人很多，你一個人出門 ___ 小心，以免上當。

   (A) 可以

   (B) 可要

   (C) 可能

   (D) 可見

41. 现在坏人很多，你一个人出门 ___ 小心，以免上当。

   (A) 可以

   (B) 可要

   (C) 可能

   (D) 可见

41. ㄒㄧㄢˋ ㄗㄞˋ ㄏㄨㄞˋ ㄖㄣˊ ㄏㄣˇ ㄉㄨㄛ ，ㄋㄧˇ ㄧ ㄍㄜ˙ ㄖㄣˊ ㄔㄨ ㄇㄣˊ ___ ㄒㄧㄠˇ ㄒㄧㄣ ，ㄧˇ ㄇㄧㄢˇ ㄕㄤˋ ㄉㄤˋ 。

   (A) ㄎㄜˇ ㄧˇ

   (B) ㄎㄜˇ ㄧㄠˋ

   (C) ㄎㄜˇ ㄋㄥˊ

   (D) ㄎㄜˇ ㄐㄧㄢˋ

41. Xiàn zài huài rén hěn duō, nǐ yí ge rén chū mén ___ xiǎo xīn, yǐ miǎn shàng dàng.

   (A) kě yǐ

   (B) kě yào

   (C) kě néng

   (D) kě jiàn

42. 天生不聰明的人____努力用功。

    (A) 不要

    (B) 更要

    (C) 只要

    (D) 必要

42. 天生不聪明的人____努力用功。

    (A) 不要

    (B) 更要

    (C) 只要

    (D) 必要

42. Tiān shēng bù cōng míng de rén,____nǔ lì yòng gōng.

    (A) bú yào

    (B) gèng yào

    (C) zhǐ yào

    (D) bì yào

43. 小高____打球很有意思。

    (A) 要是

    (B) 想要

    (C) 因爲

    (D) 覺得

43. 小高____打球很有意思。

    (A) 要是

    (B) 想要

    (C) 因为

    (D) 觉得

43. Xiǎogāo ____ dǎ qiú hěn yǒu yì si.

    (A) yào shì

    (B) xiǎng yào

    (C) yīn wèi

    (D) jué de

44. 每天早上我都要喝一杯牛奶____才出門。

    (A) 後來

    (B) 以後

    (C) 所以

    (D) 然而

44. 每天早上我都要喝一杯牛奶____才出门。

    (A) 后来

    (B) 以后

    (C) 所以

    (D) 然而

44. Měi tiān zǎo shàng wǒ dōu yào hē yì bēi niú nǎi ____ cái chū mén.

    (A) hòu lái

    (B) yǐ hòu

    (C) suǒ yǐ

    (D) rán ér

45. 走失的小孩找不到媽媽，___ 就開始大哭起來了。

    (A) 於是

    (B) 由於

    (C) 還是

    (D) 總是

45. ㄗㄡˇ ㄕ ㄉㄜ˙ ㄒㄧㄠˇ ㄏㄞˊ ㄓㄠˇ ㄅㄨˊ ㄉㄠˋ ㄇㄚ ㄇㄚ˙ ，___ ㄐㄧㄡˋ ㄎㄞ ㄕˇ ㄉㄚˋ ㄎㄨ ㄑㄧˇ ㄌㄞˊ ㄌㄜ˙ 。

    (A) ㄩˊ ㄕˋ

    (B) ㄧㄡˊ ㄩˊ

    (C) ㄏㄞˊ ㄕˋ

    (D) ㄗㄨㄥˇ ㄕˋ

45. 走失的小孩找不到妈妈，___ 就开始大哭起来了。

    (A) 於是

    (B) 由於

    (C) 还是

    (D) 总是

45. Zǒu shī de xiǎo hái zhǎo bú dào mā ma, ___ jiù kāi shǐ dà kū qǐ lái le.

    (A) yú shì

    (B) yóu yú

    (C) hái shì

    (D) zǒng shì

---

46. 他 ___ 不會唱歌，___ 不會跳舞。

    (A) 一邊…一邊

    (B) 除了…順便

    (C) 既…又

    (D) 不但…另外

46. ㄊㄚ ___ ㄅㄨˊ ㄏㄨㄟˋ ㄔㄤˋ ㄍㄜ ，___ ㄅㄨˊ ㄏㄨㄟˋ ㄊㄧㄠˋ ㄨˇ 。

    (A) ㄧ ㄅㄧㄢ … ㄧ ㄅㄧㄢ

    (B) ㄔㄨˊ ㄌㄜ˙ … ㄕㄨㄣˋ ㄅㄧㄢˋ

    (C) ㄐㄧˋ … ㄧㄡˋ

    (D) ㄅㄨˊ ㄉㄢˋ … ㄌㄧㄥˋ ㄨㄞˋ

46. 他 ___ 不会唱歌，___ 不会跳舞。

    (A) 一边…一边

    (B) 除了…顺便

    (C) 既…又

    (D) 不但…另外

46. Tā ___ bú huì chàng gē, ___ bú huì tiào wǔ.

    (A) yì biān .... yì biān

    (B) chú le .... shùn biàn

    (C) jì .... yòu

    (D) bú dàn .... lìng wài

---

47. 每次考試他 ___ 考得最好。

    (A) 總總

    (B) 總有

    (C) 總是

    (D) 總共

47. ㄇㄟˇ ㄘˋ ㄎㄠˇ ㄕˋ ㄊㄚ ___ ㄎㄠˇ ㄉㄜ˙ ㄗㄨㄟˋ ㄏㄠˇ 。

    (A) ㄗㄨㄥˇ ㄗㄨㄥˇ

    (B) ㄗㄨㄥˇ ㄧㄡˇ

    (C) ㄗㄨㄥˇ ㄕˋ

    (D) ㄗㄨㄥˇ ㄍㄨㄥˋ

47. 每次考试他 ___ 考得最好。

    (A) 总总

    (B) 总有

    (C) 总是

    (D) 总共

47. Měi cì kǎo shì tā ___ kǎo de zuì hǎo.

    (A) zǒng zǒng

    (B) zǒng yǒu

    (C) zǒng shì

    (D) zǒng gòng

48. 這本小說非常有意思，我看了都____
哈哈大笑。

    (A) 所以

    (B) 來得及

    (C) 忍不住

    (D) 最好

48. 这本小说非常有意思，我看了都____
哈哈大笑。

    (A) 所以

    (B) 来得及

    (C) 忍不住

    (D) 最好

48. ㄓㄜˋ ㄅㄣˇ ㄒㄧㄠˇ ㄕㄨㄛ ㄈㄟ ㄔㄤˊ ㄧㄡˇ ㄧ ㄙ，ㄨㄛˇ ㄎㄢˋ ㄌㄜ ㄉㄡ ____
ㄏㄚ ㄏㄚ ㄉㄚˋ ㄒㄧㄠˋ。

    (A) ㄙㄨㄛˇ ㄧˇ

    (B) ㄌㄞˊ ㄉㄜ ㄐㄧˊ

    (C) ㄖㄣˇ ㄅㄨˊ ㄓㄨˋ

    (D) ㄗㄨㄟˋ ㄏㄠˇ

48. Zhè běn xiǎo shuō fēi cháng yǒu yì si, wǒ kàn
le dōu ____ hā hā dà xiào.

    (A) suǒ yǐ

    (B) lái de jí

    (C) rěn bú zhù

    (D) zuì hǎo

---

49. 這____玫瑰花有兩打半。

    (A) 一朵

    (B) 一棵

    (C) 一束

    (D) 一枝

49. 这____玫瑰花有两打半。

    (A) 一朵

    (B) 一棵

    (C) 一束

    (D) 一枝

49. ㄓㄜˋ ____ ㄇㄟˊ ㄍㄨㄟ ㄏㄨㄚ ㄧㄡˇ ㄌㄧㄤˇ ㄉㄚˇ ㄅㄢˋ。

    (A) ㄧ ㄉㄨㄛˇ

    (B) ㄧ ㄎㄜ

    (C) ㄧˊ ㄕㄨˋ

    (D) ㄧ ㄓ

49. Zhè ____ méi guī huā yǒu liǎng dá bàn.

    (A) yì duǒ

    (B) yì kē

    (C) yí shù

    (D) yì zhī

---

50. 好久不見，妳___來___漂亮了。

    (A) 越…越

    (B) 一…是

    (C) 越…多

    (D) 更…好

50. 好久不见，妳___来___漂亮了。

    (A) 越…越

    (B) 一…是

    (C) 越…多

    (D) 更…好

50. ㄏㄠˇ ㄐㄧㄡˇ ㄅㄨˊ ㄐㄧㄢˋ，ㄋㄧˇ ___ ㄌㄞˊ ___ ㄆㄧㄠˋ ㄌㄧㄤ ㄌㄜ。

    (A) ㄩㄝˋ … ㄩㄝˋ

    (B) ㄧ … ㄕˋ

    (C) ㄩㄝˋ … ㄉㄨㄛ

    (D) ㄍㄥˋ … ㄏㄠˇ

50. Hǎo jiǔ bú jiàn, nǐ ___ lái ___ piào liang le.

    (A) yuè .... yuè

    (B) yì .... shì

    (C) yuè.... duō

    (D) gèng .... hǎo

51. 爲了付學費，他＿＿＿上學＿＿＿還要去打工。

    (A) 因爲…所以

    (B) 雖然…可是

    (C) 除了…以外

    (D) 因此…而且

51. 为了付学费，他＿＿＿上学＿＿＿还要去打工。

    (A) 因为…所以

    (B) 虽然…可是

    (C) 除了…以外

    (D) 因此…而且

51. ㄨㄟˋ ㄌㄜ˙ ㄈㄨˋ ㄒㄩㄝˊ ㄈㄟˋ，ㄊㄚ ＿＿＿ ㄕㄤˋ ㄒㄩㄝˊ ＿＿＿ ㄏㄞˊ ㄧㄠˋ ㄑㄩˋ ㄉㄚˇ ㄍㄨㄥ 。

    (A) ㄧㄣ ㄨㄟˋ … ㄙㄨㄛˇ ㄧˇ

    (B) ㄙㄨㄟ ㄖㄢˊ … ㄎㄜˇ ㄕˋ

    (C) ㄔㄨˊ ㄌㄜ˙ … ㄧˇ ㄨㄞˋ

    (D) ㄧㄣ ㄘˇ … ㄦˊ ㄑㄧㄝˇ

51. Wèi le fù xué fèi, tā ___shàng xué ___hái yào qù dǎ gōng.

    (A) yīn wèi .... suǒ yǐ

    (B) suī rán .... kě shì

    (C) chú le .... yǐ wài

    (D) yīn cǐ .... ér qiě

---

52. 下雨天去露營，＿＿＿在家看電視。

    (A) 假如

    (B) 要不是

    (C) 倒不如

    (D) 要不如

52. 下雨天去露营，＿＿＿在家看电视。

    (A) 假如

    (B) 要不是

    (C) 倒不如

    (D) 要不如

52. ㄒㄧㄚˋ ㄩˇ ㄊㄧㄢ ㄑㄩˋ ㄌㄨˋ ㄧㄥˊ，＿＿＿ ㄗㄞˋ ㄐㄧㄚ ㄎㄢˋ ㄉㄧㄢˋ ㄕˋ 。

    (A) ㄐㄧㄚˇ ㄖㄨˊ

    (B) ㄧㄠˋ ㄅㄨˋ ㄕˋ

    (C) ㄉㄠˋ ㄅㄨˋ ㄖㄨˊ

    (D) ㄧㄠˋ ㄅㄨˋ ㄖㄨˊ

52. Xià yǔ tiān qù lù yíng, ___ zài jiā kàn diàn shì.

    (A) jiǎ rú

    (B) yào bú shì

    (C) dào bù rú

    (D) yào bù rú

---

53. 他説了半天，你到底是懂＿＿＿不懂？

    (A) 不是

    (B) 還是

    (C) 也是

    (D) 但是

53. 他说了半天，你到底是懂＿＿＿不懂？

    (A) 不是

    (B) 还是

    (C) 也是

    (D) 但是

53. ㄊㄚ ㄕㄨㄛ ㄌㄜ˙ ㄅㄢˋ ㄊㄧㄢ，ㄋㄧˇ ㄉㄠˋ ㄉㄧˇ ㄕˋ ㄉㄨㄥˇ ＿＿＿ ㄅㄨˋ ㄉㄨㄥˇ ？

    (A) ㄅㄨˋ ㄕˋ

    (B) ㄏㄞˊ ㄕˋ

    (C) ㄧㄝˇ ㄕˋ

    (D) ㄉㄢˋ ㄕˋ

53. Tā shuō le bàn tiān, nǐ dào dǐ shì dǒng ___ bù dǒng?

    (A) bú shì

    (B) hái shì

    (C) yě shì

    (D) dàn shì

54. ＿＿多看書，＿＿使作文進步。

    (A) 只要…就

    (B) 只有…才能

    (C) 只要…可能

    (D) 只好…就能

54. ＿＿ㄉㄨㄛ ㄎㄢ ㄕㄨ，＿＿ㄕ ㄗㄨㄛ ㄨㄣ ㄐㄧㄣ ㄅㄨ。

    (A) ㄓ ㄠ … ㄐㄡ

    (B) ㄓ ㄡ … ㄘㄞ ㄋㄥ

    (C) ㄓ ㄠ … ㄎㄜ ㄋㄥ

    (D) ㄓ ㄠ … ㄐㄡ ㄋㄥ

54. ＿＿多看书，＿＿使作文进步。

    (A) 只要…就

    (B) 只有…才能

    (C) 只要…可能

    (D) 只好…就能

54. ＿＿ duō kàn shū, ＿＿ shǐ zuò wén jìn bù.

    (A) Zhǐ yào ... jiù

    (B) Zhǐ yǒu ... cái néng

    (C) Zhǐ yào ... kě néng

    (D) Zhǐ hǎo ... jiù néng

---

55. 大家＿＿音樂的拍子跳舞，非常愉快。

    (A) 隨著

    (B) 接著

    (C) 帶著

    (D) 靠著

55. ㄉㄚ ㄐㄧㄚ ＿＿ ㄧㄣ ㄩㄝ ㄉㄜ ㄆㄞ ㄗ ㄊㄧㄠ ㄨ，ㄈㄟ ㄔㄤ ㄩ ㄎㄨㄞ。

    (A) ㄙㄨㄟ ㄓㄜ

    (B) ㄐㄧㄝ ㄓㄜ

    (C) ㄉㄞ ㄓㄜ

    (D) ㄎㄠ ㄓㄜ

55. 大家＿＿音乐的拍子跳舞，非常愉快。

    (A) 随著

    (B) 接著

    (C) 带著

    (D) 靠著

55. Dà jiā ＿＿ yīn yuè de pāi zi tiào wǔ, fēi cháng yú kuài.

    (A) suí zhe

    (B) jiē zhe

    (C) dài zhe

    (D) kào zhe

SAT II 中文模擬試題 第二套
Section III : Reading Comprehension

Directions: Read the following selections carefully for comprehension. Each selection is followed by one or more questions or incomplete statements based on its content. Select the answer or completion that is best according to the passage and fill in the corresponding oval on the answer sheet.
THIS SECTION OF THE TEST IS PRESENTED IN TWO WRITING SYSTEMS: TRADITIONAL CHARACTERS AND SIMPLIFIED CHARACTERS. IT IS RECOMMENDED THAT YOU CHOOSE ONLY THAT WRITING SYSTEM WITH WHICH YOU ARE MOST FAMILIAR AS YOU WORK THROUGH THIS SECTION OF THE TEST.

56~57

哥哥以前在臺灣上到小學三年級，學會了很多中文，會讀也會寫，可是到了美國以後，哥哥把很多中文都忘了。

不過我們的祖母規定我們在家時，只可說中文，所以哥哥還會說一些中文。

雖然哥哥現在都上高中了，才開始再學中文，但是〝活到老，學到老〞，永遠都不會太遲。

哥哥以前在台湾上到小学三年级，学会了很多中文，会读也会写，可是到了美国以后，哥哥把很多中文都忘了。

不过我们的祖母规定我们在家时，只可说中文，所以哥哥还会说一些中文。

虽然哥哥现在都上高中了，才开始再学中文，但是〝活到老，学到老〞，永远都不会太迟。

Question 56
Where did his brother come from?
(A) U.S.A.
(B) Mainland China
(C) Hong Kong
(D) Taiwan

Question 57
What is the meaning of 〝活到老，學到老〞?
(A) He will study tonight.
(B) He will go to Taiwan to study.
(C) Never stop learning.
(D) He will go to Chinese school to learn Chinese.

58

中央圖書館
開放時間
星期一至星期五　上午八點至晚上九點
星期六　　　　　上午十點至下午六點
星期日　　　　　下午一點至五點
國定假日休息

中央图书馆
开放时间
星期一至星期五　上午八点至晚上九点
星期六　　　　　上午十点至下午六点
星期日　　　　　下午一点至五点
国定假日休息

Question 58　This library is

(A)　open 8:00am - 9:00pm on Saturdays

(B)　closed on holidays

(C)　closed on Sunday afternoons

(D)　open everyday from 8:00am - 6:00pm

59~60

超級六合彩
四月二十六日開獎
3　5　11
26　35　47
獎金2200萬元

超级六合彩
四月二十六日开奖
3　5　11
26　35　47
奖金2200万元

Question 59　This is

(A)　a lottery ticket

(B)　a bus ticket

(C)　a movie ticket

(D)　a concert ticket

Question 60　How much will you get if you pick 6 correct numbers?

(A)　$22,000

(B)　$220,000

(C)　$2,200,000

(D)　$22,000,000

61

敬愛的老師：

　　謝謝您的關心與教導。祝您

教師節快樂！

　　　　學生

　　　　　　多多敬上

　　　　八十八年九月二十八日

敬爱的老师：

　　谢谢您的关心与教导。祝您

教师节快乐！

　　　　学生

　　　　　　多多敬上

　　　　八十八年九月二十八日

Question 61　　　This is

(A)　　a thank you card for a student

(B)　　a thank you card from a teacher

(C)　　a thank you card for a teacher's day

(D)　　a thank you card for a birthday gift

62~63

天氣預告

5月28日　　　星期日

晨霧轉晴　　　50/68

天气预告

5月28日　　　星期日

晨雾转晴　　　50/68

Question 62　　　This is the information for a

(A)　　movie schedule

(B)　　weather forecast

(C)　　TV program

(D)　　radio program

Question 63　　　May 28 is a

(A)　　Sunday

(B)　　Thursday

(C)　　Wednesday

(D)　　Saturday

64~65

這類襯衫的顏色種類那麼多，我該挑什麼顏色才好，紅色太艷了，送她紫色的，也許比較適合。

这类衬衫的颜色种类那麼多，我该挑什么颜色才好，红色太艳了，送她紫色的，也许比较适合。

Question 64 What is this person trying to get?

(A) a blouse

(B) some pants

(C) a coat

(D) a hat

Question 65 What color might he choose?

(A) red

(B) purple

(C) green

(D) brown

66

上次我公司裏的同事在這兒訂做了一件旗袍，也是遇到這種不能按期交貨的情況，你們真該想點辦法啊！時間是寶貴的，您總不能要客人天天往這裏跑。

上次我公司里的同事在这儿訂做了一件旗袍，也是遇到这种不能按期交货的情况，你们真该想点办法啊！时间是宝贵的，您总不能要客人天天往这裏跑。

Question 66 Why can't customers keep coming every day?

(A) Customers are very tired.

(B) Customers will travel to Europe.

(C) Customers have their computer classes.

(D) Time is precious, so customers shouldn't waste time.

五月的第二個星期日是母親節。那一天，一般的傳統是母親尚健在的人都會在胸前別上一朵紅色的康乃馨，母親已經去世的人就會別上白色的。

媽媽和我還有妹妹，我們在那一天都很高興的戴上紅色的康乃馨，只有爸爸的胸前戴的是白色的康乃馨。

五月的第二个星期日是母亲节。那一天，一般的传统是母亲尚健在的人都会在胸前别上一朵红色的康乃馨，母亲已经去世的人就会别上白色的。

妈妈和我还有妹妹，我们在那一天都很高兴的戴上红色的康乃馨，只有爸爸的胸前戴的是白色的康乃馨。

Question 67   What's special about the second Sunday of May?

(A)   It's Mother's Day.

(B)   It's the start of summer.

(C)   It's Father's Day.

(D)   It's Grandparent's Day.

Question 68   Whose mother is no longer alive?

(A)   someone else's

(B)   the mother's

(C)   the father's

(D)   the author's

Question 69   How many people are there in the author's immediate family?

(A)   3

(B)   4

(C)   5

(D)   6

70

非常抱歉！王教授，您今天早晨要
用的參考書，我沒有全部準備好，
一定使您為難了吧！請原諒！

非常抱歉！王教授，您今天早晨要
用的参考书，我没有全部准备好，
一定使您为难了吧！请原谅！

Question 70   What was the speaker sorry about?

(A)   getting up very late this morning

(B)   not writing the report this morning

(C)   missing the morning bus

(D)   not getting ready all the reference books

71~73

電腦公司誠徵
司機
需工作勤快，有良好駕駛記錄
請電：510-263-5000

电脑公司诚徵
司机
需工作勤快，有良好驾驶记录
请电：510-263-5000

Question 71   What is this company looking for?

(A)   a salesman

(B)   a technician

(C)   an operator

(D)   a driver

Question 72   What kind of company is this?

(A)   an insurance company

(B)   a shipping company

(C)   a computer company

(D)   a telephone company

Question 73 What qualifications must the applicant have?

(A) a BS degree with a good driving record

(B) a BS degree with good computer knowledge

(C) know how to fix cars

(D) work hard with a good driving record

 # 74~75

我習慣每天早上看報紙。因為時間有限，我只看一看標題。報上登的，除了政治、外交、經濟、教育、文化令我感興趣的新聞外，還有我最喜歡的是看有關體育活動的消息。

我习惯每天早上看报纸。因为时间有限，我只看一看标题。报上登的，除了政治、外交、经济、教育、文化令我感兴趣的新闻外，还有我最喜欢的是看有关体育活动的消息。

Question 74 What does〝標題〞mean？

(A) a punctuation mark

(B) a standard

(C) a headline

(D) a target

Question 75 How many sections do I read in the newspaper?

(A) 4

(B) 5

(C) 6

(D) 7

要學騎自行車很容易，一個上午就能學會。學會了騎車，週末便可以和朋友一起去郊外玩。

要学骑自行车很容易，一个上午就能学会。学会了骑车，周末便可以和朋友一起去郊外玩。

Question 76　　What is this paragraph about?

(A)　driving a car

(B)　riding a bus

(C)　riding a motorcycle

(D)　riding a bicycle

77

媽媽今天早上給我 $4.50 吃午飯。以下是學校今天自助餐廳的菜單：

①三明治（兩塊）
②沙拉　　（一塊七毛五）
③意大利通心粉（兩塊五毛五）
④炸雞　（一塊八毛五）
⑤中式炒飯（兩塊）

　　（以上價錢均已含稅）

妈妈今天早上给我 $4.50 吃午饭。以下是学校今天自助餐厅的菜单：

①三明治（两块）
②沙拉　　（一块七毛五）
③意大利通心粉（两块五毛五）
④炸鸡　（一块八毛五）
⑤中式炒饭（两块）

　　（以上价钱均已含税）

Question 77　　Which two combinations will leave you with the least amount of money?

(A)　①⑤

(B)　③④

(C)　①③

(D)　②④

 # 78

如何寫中式信封：先寫收信人的
地址，然後把收信人的姓名寫在信
封的中間，最後把寄信人的地址和
姓名寫在左下方。

如何写中式信封：先写收信人的地
址，然后把收信人的姓名写在信封
的中间，最后把寄信人的地址和姓
名写在左下方。

Question 78 Where do you write the recipient's name?

(A) on the bottom right of the envelope

(B) in the middle of the envelope

(C) at the top left of the envelope

(D) on the bottom left of the envelope

 # 79

注意：離開房間，勿忘關燈

注意：离开房间，勿忘关灯

Question 79 What is this warning about?

(A) Turn on the music before you leave.

(B) Turn off the light before you leave.

(C) Turn off the stove before you leave.

(D) Turn off the stove after you cook.

 # 80

Question 80 What does this sign mean?

(A) public bath

(B) private bath

(C) public lavatory

(D) private lavatory

64

81

遊人止步，請走東門

游人止步，请走东门

Question 81   Which gate is for visitors?

    (A)   north gate

    (B)   south gate

    (C)   east gate

    (D)   west gate

82

通告

所有持有圖書館書的學生，請在下課後到101教室集合。

通告

所有持有图书馆书的学生，请在下课后到101教室集合。

Question 82   Who should go to room 101?

    (A)   all students

    (B)   all teachers

    (C)   all students with overdue books

    (D)   all students with library books

83

用法：
滴入眼瞼內，一次1～2滴，一日3～5次。

用法：
滴入眼瞼内，一次1～2滴，一日3～5次。

Question 83   According to the instructions, what's the maximum number of drops a day?

    (A)   3 drops

    (B)   6 drops

    (C)   5 drops

    (D)   10 drops

84

【人體 保健食譜】，由文化出
版社出版，定價每冊20元，郵購
加郵費10%，歡迎訂購。

【人体 保健食谱】，由文化出
版社出版，定价每册20元，邮购
加邮费10%，欢迎订购。

Question 84   How much do I have to pay for 2 mail orders?

(A) $ 38

(B) $ 40

(C) $ 44

(D) $ 42

85

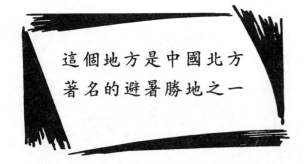

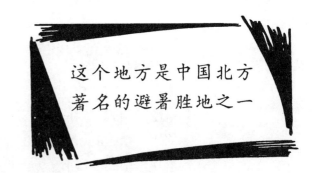

Question 85   When is the best time to go there?

(A)   spring

(B)   summer

(C)   fall

(D)   winter

SAT II 中文模擬試卷 第三套
Section I : Listening Comprehension

Part A

Directions: In this part of the test you will hear short questions, statements, or exchanges in Mandarin Chinese, follow by three responses designated (A), (B), and (C). You will hear the statements or questions, as well as the responses, just one time and they are not printed in your test booklet. Therefore, you must listen very carefully. Select the best response and fill in the corresponding oval on your answer sheet. You will have 15 seconds to answer each question.

Question 1	(A)	(B)	(C)
Question 2	(A)	(B)	(C)
Question 3	(A)	(B)	(C)
Question 4	(A)	(B)	(C)
Question 5	(A)	(B)	(C)
Question 6	(A)	(B)	(C)
Question 7	(A)	(B)	(C)
Question 8	(A)	(B)	(C)
Question 9	(A)	(B)	(C)
Question 10	(A)	(B)	(C)
Question 11	(A)	(B)	(C)
Question 12	(A)	(B)	(C)
Question 13	(A)	(B)	(C)
Question 14	(A)	(B)	(C)
Question 15	(A)	(B)	(C)

Part B

Directions: You will now hear a series of short selections. You will hear them <u>only once</u> and they are not printed in your test booklet. After each selection, you will be asked one or more questions about what you have just heard. These questions, with four possible answers, are printed in your test booklet. Select the best answer to each question from among the four choices given and fill in the corresponding oval on your answer sheet. You will have 15 seconds to answer each question.

 # 16

<u>Question 16</u>   Which of the following statements is true?

      (A)   The three people are most likely in the speaker's house.

      (B)   The speaker thinks that Mr. Wang and Mr. Lin are old friends.

      (C)   Mr. Wang told Mr. Lin that he works in the school.

      (D)   The speaker told Mr. Wang that Mr. Lin works in the library.

 # 17~18

<u>Question 17</u>   Which of the following statements is true?

      (A)   The woman hopes to attend the dance at the man's school.

      (B)   The woman hopes to attend a tea party at the man's school.

      (C)   The woman invites the man to join a dinner party at her school.

      (D)   The woman invites the man to attend a dance at her school.

<u>Question 18</u>   What was the excuse?

      (A)   There is another dinner party to attend.

      (B)   There is a tea party on Monday.

      (C)   There is a test on Monday.

      (D)   There is another party to attend on Sunday night.

 # 19~20

<u>Question 19</u>   What date is today?

      (A)   Oct. 4

      (B)   Oct. 10

      (C)   April 4

      (D)   April 10

<u>Question 20</u>   What day is today?

      (A)   Wednesday

      (B)   Thursday

      (C)   Friday

      (D)   Saturday

 # 21~23

Question 21   When did the woman buy the skirt?

(A)   last week

(B)   two days ago

(C)   yesterday

(D)   Thursday

Question 22   What does the woman not like about the skirt?

(A)   style

(B)   size

(C)   color

(D)   size and color

Question 23   What color does the salesperson say are available?

(A)   yellow, white and blue

(B)   red, white and blue

(C)   brown, blue and white

(D)   pink, blue and white

 # 24~25

Question 24   Which of the following statements is true?

(A)   A ticket will be mailed.

(B)   He will attend an overseas tour.

(C)   He is booking a plane ticket.

(D)   He is planning a business trip.

Question 25   Where will the person change planes and stay for one night?

(A)   New York

(B)   Los Angeles

(C)   Chicago

(D)   none of the above

 # 26~28

Question 26   What is Miss Chen's occupation?

(A)   a teacher

(B)   a student

(C)   a helper

(D)   a store manager

Question 27   How often does Miss Chen visit the senior center?

(A)   once a month

(B)   once a week

(C)   twice a week

(D)   every two weeks

Question 28   What are they planning to do tomorrow?

(A)   see a movie

(B)   go shopping

(C)   play tennis

(D)   visit the senior center

 # 29~30

Question 29   Where does this conversation take place?

(A)   in a shopping mall

(B)   in a car

(C)   in a supermarket

(D)   in a concert

Question 30   How much will they spend on parking?

(A)   1 dollar

(B)   2 dollars

(C)   3 dollars

(D)   4 dollars

SAT II 中文模擬試題 第三套
Section I : Listening Comprehension

Part A

Directions: In this part of the test you will hear short questions, statements, or exchanges in Mandarin Chinese, followed by three responses designated (A), (B), and (C). You will hear the statements or questions, as well as the responses, just one time and they are not printed in your test booklet. Therefore, you must listen very carefully. Select the best response and fill in the corresponding oval on your answer sheet. You will have 15 seconds to answer each question.

Question 1

白小姐，妳的中國話說得真好。

 (A) 哪裏，還差得遠呢！

 (B) 太麻煩你了。

 (C) 謝謝，我自己來。

Question 2

你星期六幾點鐘請吃晚飯？

 (A) 星期六晚上見。

 (B) 六點鐘，怎麼樣？

 (C) 星期六我很忙。

Question 3

王先生會哪些外語？

 (A) 他對學外語很有興趣。

 (B) 德語和法語。

 (C) 他學過一年外語。

Question 4

你看醫生了嗎？

 (A) 是嗎？

 (B) 沒有。

 (C) 體溫很高。

Question 5

這本書多少錢？

 (A) 很便宜。

 (B) 兩塊錢。

 (C) 四點五分。

Question 6

請問哪兒有加油站？

 (A) 我沒有零錢。

 (B) 沒問題，車子還有油。

 (C) 右前方不遠的地方。

Question 7

想喝點什麼？喜歡咖啡嗎？
      (A) 謝謝！我不喝茶。
      (B) 我不喝啤酒，請給我一杯茶吧！
      (C) 我不喝咖啡，請給我一杯茶吧！

Question 8

小高，快放暑假了，你打算做什麼？
      (A) 我去過紐約。
      (B) 我從紐約來的。
      (C) 我要去紐約旅行。

Question 9

下午我們去看電影，好嗎？
      (A) 好啊！我們去看三點一刻的那一場。
      (B) 那部電影很好看，我下午去看過了。
      (C) 我們現在可以回家了。

Question 10

你去過<u>中國</u>嗎？
      (A) 我沒有去過。
      (B) 我喜歡過中國年。
      (C) 我喜歡中國城。

Question 11

我們今天晚上吃中餐還是西餐？
      (A) 我們開車去吃。
      (B) 吃中餐。
      (C) 西餐比中餐貴。

Question 12

你會滑雪嗎？

    (A)我喜歡滑雪。

    (B)會一點。

    (C)雪地的風景很美。

Question 13

先生，請問到漁人碼頭怎麼走？

    (A)先往前走，到紅綠燈的時候向右轉。

    (B)漁人碼頭的東西很貴。

    (C)走到漁人碼頭大約要十分鐘。

Question 14

哇！你的黑車好漂亮啊！

    (A)我要開去聖荷西。

    (B)黑色是我最喜歡的顏色。

    (C)天黑開車很危險。

Question 15

我們下午一點一塊兒吃中飯，好嗎？

    (A)我要開會，晚一個鐘頭好了。

    (B)請你吃快一點兒。

    (C)開會時間到了。

Part B

Directions: You will now hear a series of short selections. You will hear them <u>only once</u> and they are not printed in your test booklet. After each selection, you will be asked one or more questions about what you have just heard. These questions, with four possible answers, are printed in your test booklet. Select the best answer to each question from among the four choices given and fill in the corresponding oval on your answer sheet. You will have 15 seconds to answer each question.

Question 16

請進請進，我給你們介紹一下。這是我的朋友王先生。這是林先生，他在書店工作。

Question 17~18

女：小劉，星期天晚上，請你來參加我們學校的舞會，好嗎？

男：謝謝你！星期天晚上我不行，因為我星期一要考試。

Question 19~20

女：今天是四月十號嗎？

男：是的，沒錯，今天是四月十號。

女：今天是星期幾呢？

男：今天是星期三。

Question 21~23

男：太太，您想買什麼嗎？

女：我昨天買了一件中號的紅色裙子太大了。

男：想換小號的嗎？

女：是的，我也想換顏色。

男：沒問題，我可以給您換件小號的。這件藍色的怎麼樣？

女：我覺得顏色太暗了。有沒有黃色的？

男：對不起，這種裙子只有紅、白、藍三種顏色。

女：那就給我白的吧！

Question 24~25

男：亞洲旅行社嗎？我想訂一張機票。

女：請問你要去那兒？

男：我想先從紐約飛芝加哥，在那兒轉機，停留一天，然後再飛洛杉磯。

女：好。

Question 26~28

女：李先生，你好！好久不見了。

男：喔！陳小姐，妳好！最近還去當義工嗎？

女：是啊！自從到學校教書以後，我一個星期去一次。

男：林奶奶還住在老人中心嗎？

女：是的！她和張奶奶、王爺爺都還住在那兒。

男：我很想念他們。我們明天一起去看他們，好嗎？

女：好啊！

Question 29~30

女：音樂會馬上就要開始了，這附近已經沒有免費的停車位了。

男：喔！對面有付錢的停車場，我們可以停在那兒。

女：一個小時一塊錢，一個晚上三塊錢，還不算太貴。我們趕快去停車。

SAT II 中文模擬試題 第三套
Section II : Grammar

Directions: This section consists of a number of incomplete statements, each of which has four suggested completions. Select the word or phrase that best completes the sentence structurally and logically. Please fill in the corresponding oval on the answer sheet.

THE QUESTIONS ARE PRESENTED IN FOUR DIFFERENT WRITING SYSTEMS: TRADITIONAL CHARACTERS, SIMPLIFIED CHARACTERS, PINYIN ROMANIZATION, AND CHINESE PHONETIC ALPHABET(BO PO MO FO). TO SAVE TIME, IT IS RECOMMENDED THAT YOU CHOOSE THE WRITING SYSTEM WITH WHICH YOU ARE MOST FAMILIAR WITH AND **READ ONLY THAT VERSION OF THE QUESTION.**

31. 今天外面很冷，你最好__上大衣。

    (A) 用
    (B) 穿
    (C) 放
    (D) 戴

31. 今天外面很冷，你最好__上大衣。

    (A) 用
    (B) 穿
    (C) 放
    (D) 戴

31. ㄐㄧㄣ ㄊㄧㄢ ㄨㄞ ㄇㄧㄢ ㄏㄣ ㄌㄥ，ㄋㄧ ㄗㄨㄟ ㄏㄠ __ ㄕㄤ ㄉㄚ ㄧ 。

    (A) ㄩㄥ
    (B) ㄔㄨㄢ
    (C) ㄈㄤ
    (D) ㄉㄞ

31. Jīn tiān wài miàn hěn lěng, nǐ zuì hǎo__shàng dà yī.

    (A) yòng
    (B) chuān
    (C) fàng
    (D) dài

---

32. 請你___門關好。

    (A) 帶
    (B) 把
    (C) 替
    (D) 被

32. 请你___门关好。

    (A) 带
    (B) 把
    (C) 替
    (D) 被

32. ㄑㄧㄥ ㄋㄧ ___ ㄇㄣ ㄍㄨㄢ ㄏㄠ 。

    (A) ㄉㄞ
    (B) ㄅㄚ
    (C) ㄊㄧ
    (D) ㄅㄟ

32. Qǐng nǐ ___ mén guān hǎo.

    (A) dài
    (B) bǎ
    (C) tì
    (D) bèi

33. 他 ___ 有空 ___ 喜歡看書。

    (A) 這…都

    (B) 從…到

    (C) 是…得

    (D) 一…就

33. ㄊ ___ ㄧㄡ ㄎㄨㄥ ___ ㄒㄧ ㄏㄨㄢ ㄎㄢ ㄕㄨ 。

    (A) ㄓㄜ … ㄉㄡ

    (B) ㄘㄨㄥ … ㄉㄠ

    (C) ㄕ … ㄉㄜ

    (D) ㄧ … ㄐㄧㄡ

33. 他 ___ 有空 ___ 喜欢看书。

    (A) 这…都

    (B) 从…到

    (C) 是…得

    (D) 一…就

33. Tā ___ yǒu kòng ___ xǐ huān kàn shū.

    (A) zhè .... dōu

    (B) cóng .... dào

    (C) shì .... de

    (D) yì .... jiù

---

34. 我不喜歡這部電影，你 ___？

    (A) 啊

    (B) 嗎

    (C) 呢

    (D) 吧

34. ㄨㄛ ㄅㄨ ㄒㄧ ㄏㄨㄢ ㄓㄜ ㄅㄨ ㄉㄧㄢ ㄧㄥ ，ㄋㄧ ___？

    (A) ㄚ

    (B) ㄇㄚ

    (C) ㄋㄜ

    (D) ㄅㄚ

34. 我不喜欢这部电影，你 ___？

    (A) 啊

    (B) 吗

    (C) 呢

    (D) 吧

34. Wǒ bù xǐ huān zhè bù diàn yǐng, nǐ ___ ?

    (A) a

    (B) ma

    (C) ne

    (D) ba

---

35. 你怎麼 ___ 遲到了？

    (A) 才

    (B) 再

    (C) 又

    (D) 只

35. ㄋㄧ ㄗㄣ ㄇㄜ ___ ㄔ ㄉㄠ ㄌㄜ？

    (A) ㄘㄞ

    (B) ㄗㄞ

    (C) ㄧㄡ

    (D) ㄓ

35. 你怎么 ___ 迟到了？

    (A) 才

    (B) 再

    (C) 又

    (D) 只

35. Nǐ zěn me ___ chí dào le?

    (A) cái

    (B) zài

    (C) yòu

    (D) zhǐ

36. 除了王先生 ___ ，其他的人都來了。

    (A) 以上

    (B) 以下

    (C) 以外

    (D) 以內

36. 除了王先生 ___ ，其他的人都来了。

    (A) 以上

    (B) 以下

    (C) 以外

    (D) 以內

36. ㄔㄨˊ ㄌㄜ˙ ㄨㄤˊ ㄒㄧㄢ ㄕㄥ ___ ，ㄑㄧˊ ㄊㄚ ㄉㄜ˙ ㄖㄣˊ ㄉㄡ ㄌㄞˊ ㄌㄜ˙ 。

    (A) ㄧˇ ㄕㄤˋ

    (B) ㄧˇ ㄒㄧㄚˋ

    (C) ㄧˇ ㄨㄞˋ

    (D) ㄧˇ ㄋㄟˋ

36. Chú le Wáng xiān sheng ___ , qí tā de rén dōu lái le.

    (A) yǐ shàng

    (B) yǐ xià

    (C) yǐ wài

    (D) yǐ nèi

---

37. 因爲沒帶錢，___ 不吃了。

    (A) 只會

    (B) 只要

    (C) 只是

    (D) 只好

37. 因为没带钱，___ 不吃了。

    (A) 只会

    (B) 只要

    (C) 只是

    (D) 只好

37. ㄧㄣ ㄨㄟˋ ㄇㄟˊ ㄉㄞˋ ㄑㄧㄢˊ ，___ ㄅㄨˋ ㄔ ㄌㄜ˙ 。

    (A) ㄓˇ ㄏㄨㄟˋ

    (B) ㄓˇ ㄧㄠˋ

    (C) ㄓˇ ㄕˋ

    (D) ㄓˇ ㄏㄠˇ

37. Yīn wèi méi dài qián, ___ bù chī le.

    (A) zhǐ huì

    (B) zhǐ yào

    (C) zhǐ shì

    (D) zhǐ hǎo

---

38. 這衣服的顏色 _____ ？

    (A) 怎麼會

    (B) 什麼樣

    (C) 怎麼樣

    (D) 什麼是

38. 这衣服的颜色 _____ ？

    (A) 怎么会

    (B) 什么样

    (C) 怎么样

    (D) 什么是

38. ㄓㄜˋ ㄧ ㄈㄨˊ ㄉㄜ˙ ㄧㄢˊ ㄙㄜˋ _____ ？

    (A) ㄗㄣˇ ㄇㄜ˙ ㄏㄨㄟˋ

    (B) ㄕㄣˊ ㄇㄜ˙ ㄧㄤˋ

    (C) ㄗㄣˇ ㄇㄜ˙ ㄧㄤˋ

    (D) ㄕㄣˊ ㄇㄜ˙ ㄕˋ

38. Zhè yī fú de yán sè _____ ？

    (A) zěn me huì

    (B) shén me yàng

    (C) zěn me yàng

    (D) shén me shì

39. 因爲我生病了，所以 ___ 去上學。

    (A) 可是

    (B) 可能

    (C) 不能

    (D) 可以

39. 因为我生病了，所以 ___ 去上学。

    (A) 可是

    (B) 可能

    (C) 不能

    (D) 可以

39. ㄣ ㄟ ㄜ ㄖ ㄓ ㄌ ，ㄜ ㄧ ___ ㄙ ㄓ ㄜ 。

    (A) ㄜ ㄕ

    (B) ㄜ ㄋ

    (C) ㄨ ㄋ

    (D) ㄜ ㄧ

39. Yīn wèi wǒ shēng bìng le, suǒ yǐ _____ qù shàng xué.

    (A) kě shì

    (B) kě néng

    (C) bù néng

    (D) kě yǐ

40. 我從來沒吃 ___ 這麼好吃的東西。

    (A) 得

    (B) 過

    (C) 給

    (D) 成

40. 我从来没吃 ___ 这麼好吃的东西。

    (A) 得

    (B) 过

    (C) 给

    (D) 成

40. ㄜ ㄌ ㄨ ㄔ ___ ㄓ ㄜ ㄠ ㄔ ㄜ ㄉ 。

    (A) ㄜ

    (B) ㄜ

    (C) ㄟ

    (D) ㄜ

40. Wǒ cóng lái méi chī ___ zhè me hǎo chī de dōng xi.

    (A) de

    (B) guò

    (C) gěi

    (D) chéng

41. 請問圖書館在 ____ ?

    (A) 什麼

    (B) 那麼

    (C) 那兒

    (D) 這麼

41. 请问图书馆在 ____ ?

    (A) 什么

    (B) 那么

    (C) 那儿

    (D) 这么

41. ㄑ ㄨ ㄊ ㄕ ㄍ ㄗ ____ ?

    (A) ㄕ ㄜ

    (B) ㄋ ㄜ

    (C) ㄋ 儿

    (D) ㄓ ㄜ

41. Qǐng wèn tú shū guǎn zài ____ ?

    (A) shén me

    (B) nà me

    (C) nǎr

    (D) zhè me

42. 那本中文書 ____ 李小姐借走了。

    (A) 把

    (B) 拿

    (C) 被

    (D) 使

42. 那本中文书 ____ 李小姐借走了。

    (A) 把

    (B) 拿

    (C) 被

    (D) 使

42. Nà běn zhōngwén shū ____ Lǐ xiǎo jiě jiè zǒu le.

    (A) bǎ

    (B) ná

    (C) bèi

    (D) shǐ

---

43. 你如果沒空，我可以___你去還書。

    (A) 要

    (B) 替

    (C) 被

    (D) 向

43. 你如果没空，我可以___你去还书。

    (A) 要

    (B) 替

    (C) 被

    (D) 向

43. Nǐ rú guǒ méi kòng, wǒ kě yǐ ____ nǐ qù huán shū.

    (A) yào

    (B) tì

    (C) bèi

    (D) xiàng

---

44. ____哥哥比我大五歲，____我比哥哥高。

    (A) 因爲 … 所以

    (B) 既然 … 就

    (C) 雖然 … 但是

    (D) 就是 … 也

44. ____哥哥比我大五岁，____我比哥哥高。

    (A) 因为 … 所以

    (B) 既然 … 就

    (C) 虽然 … 但是

    (D) 就是 … 也

44. ____ gē ge bǐ wǒ dà wǔ suì, ____ wǒ bǐ gē ge gāo.

    (A) Yīn wèi .... suǒ yǐ

    (B) Jì rán .... jiù

    (C) Suī rán .... dàn shì

    (D) Jiù shì .... yě

45. 他在美國＿＿＿住了十年了。

    (A) 已經
    (B) 經過
    (C) 經常
    (D) 常常

45. ㄊㄚ ㄗㄞˋ ㄇㄟˇ ㄍㄨㄛˊ＿＿＿ㄓㄨˋ ㄌㄜ˙ ㄕˊ ㄋㄧㄢˊ ㄌㄜ˙ 。

    (A) ㄧˇ ㄐㄧㄥ
    (B) ㄐㄧㄥ ㄍㄨㄛˋ
    (C) ㄐㄧㄥ ㄔㄤˊ
    (D) ㄔㄤˊ ㄔㄤˊ

45. 他在美国＿＿＿住了十年了。

    (A) 已经
    (B) 经过
    (C) 经常
    (D) 常常

45. Tā zài Měiguó ＿＿＿ zhù le shí nián le.

    (A) yǐ jīng
    (B) jīng guò
    (C) jīng cháng
    (D) cháng cháng

---

46. 他 ＿＿＿ 音樂有興趣。

    (A) 吧
    (B) 給
    (C) 對
    (D) 向

46. ㄊㄚ ＿＿＿ ㄧㄣ ㄩㄝˋ ㄧㄡˇ ㄒㄧㄥˋ ㄑㄩˋ 。

    (A) ㄅㄚ˙
    (B) ㄍㄟˇ
    (C) ㄉㄨㄟˋ
    (D) ㄒㄧㄤˋ

46. 他 ＿＿＿ 音乐有兴趣。

    (A) 吧
    (B) 给
    (C) 对
    (D) 向

46. Tā ＿＿＿ yīn yuè yǒu xìng qù.

    (A) ba
    (B) gěi
    (C) duì
    (D) xiàng

---

47. 小明 ＿＿＿ 去 ＿＿＿ 紐約。

    (A) 昨天…来
    (B) 曾經…過
    (C) 是…只有
    (D) 不再…来

47. ㄒㄧㄠˇ ㄇㄧㄥˊ ＿＿＿ ㄑㄩˋ ＿＿＿ ㄋㄧㄡˇ ㄩㄝ 。

    (A) ㄗㄨㄛˊ ㄊㄧㄢ … ㄌㄞˊ
    (B) ㄘㄥˊ ㄐㄧㄥ … ㄍㄨㄛˋ
    (C) ㄕˋ … ㄓˇ ㄧㄡˇ
    (D) ㄅㄨˊ ㄗㄞˋ … ㄌㄞˊ

47. 小明 ＿＿＿ 去 ＿＿＿ 纽约。

    (A) 昨天…来
    (B) 曾经…过
    (C) 是…只有
    (D) 不再…来

47. Xiǎomíng ＿＿＿ qù ＿＿＿ Niǔyuē.

    (A) zuó tiān .... lái
    (B) céng jīng .... guò
    (C) shì .... zhǐ yǒu
    (D) bú zài .... lái

48. 他 ___ 早飯 ___ 沒吃，就去上學了。

    (A) 一…就

    (B) 連…都

    (C) 雖然…但是

    (D) 不跟…一樣

48. ㄊㄚ ___ ㄗㄠˇㄈㄢˋ ___ ㄇㄟˊㄔ，ㄐㄧㄡˋㄑㄩˋㄕㄤˋㄒㄩㄝˊㄌㄜ。

    (A) ㄧ … ㄐㄧㄡˋ

    (B) ㄌㄧㄢˊ … ㄉㄡ

    (C) ㄙㄨㄟ ㄖㄢˊ … ㄉㄢˋㄕˋ

    (D) ㄅㄨˋㄍㄣ … ㄧˊㄧㄤˋ

48. 他 ___ 早饭 ___ 没吃，就去上学了。

    (A) 一…就

    (B) 连…都

    (C) 虽然…但是

    (D) 不跟…一样

48. Tā ___ zǎo fàn ___ méi chī, jiù qù shàng xué le.

    (A) yī .... jiù

    (B) lián ....dōu

    (C) suī rán .... dàn shì

    (D) bù gēn .... yí yàng

49. 他們 _____ 用做中文功課 ___ 。

    (A) 再也不…明天

    (B) 明天不…完

    (C) 再也不…了

    (D) 今天不…完

49. ㄊㄚ ㄇㄣ _____ ㄩㄥˋㄗㄨㄛˋㄓㄨㄥㄨㄣˊㄍㄨㄥㄎㄜˋ ___ 。

    (A) ㄗㄞˋㄧㄝˇㄅㄨˊ … ㄇㄧㄥˊㄊㄧㄢ

    (B) ㄇㄧㄥˊㄊㄧㄢㄅㄨˊ … ㄨㄢˊ

    (C) ㄗㄞˋㄧㄝˇㄅㄨˊ … ㄌㄜ

    (D) ㄐㄧㄣㄊㄧㄢㄅㄨˊ … ㄨㄢˊ

49. 他们 _____ 用做中文功课 ___ 。

    (A) 再也不…明天

    (B) 明天不…完

    (C) 再也不…了

    (D) 今天不…完

49. Tā men ___ yòng zuò Zhōngwén gōng kè __ .

    (A) zài yě bú .... míng tiān

    (B) míng tiān bú .... wán

    (C) zài yě bú .... le

    (D) jīn tiān bú .... wán

50. 他們 ___ 衝到一塊大石頭旁邊。

    (A) 帶

    (B) 被

    (C) 把

    (D) 有

50. ㄊㄚ ㄇㄣ ___ ㄔㄨㄥ ㄉㄠˋㄧˊㄎㄨㄞˋㄉㄚˋㄕˊㄊㄡˊㄆㄤˊㄅㄧㄢ 。

    (A) ㄉㄞˋ

    (B) ㄅㄟˋ

    (C) ㄅㄚˇ

    (D) ㄧㄡˇ

50. 他们 ___ 冲到一块大石头旁边。

    (A) 带

    (B) 被

    (C) 把

    (D) 有

50. Tā men ___ chōng dào yí kuài dà shí tóu páng biān.

    (A) dài

    (B) bèi

    (C) bǎ

    (D) yǒu

51. 早上還有太陽，下午卻___下雨了。

    (A) 不然

    (B) 雖然

    (C) 忽然

    (D) 當然

51. 早上还有太阳，下午却___下雨了。

    (A) 不然

    (B) 虽然

    (C) 忽然

    (D) 当然

51. ㄗㄠ ㄕㄤ ㄏㄞ ㄧㄡ ㄊㄞ ㄧㄤ，ㄒㄧㄚ ㄨ ㄑㄩㄝ ___ㄒㄧㄚ ㄩ ㄌㄜ。

    (A) ㄅㄨ ㄖㄢ

    (B) ㄙㄨㄟ ㄖㄢ

    (C) ㄏㄨ ㄖㄢ

    (D) ㄉㄤ ㄖㄢ

51. Zǎo shàng hái yǒu tài yáng, xià wǔ què ___xià yǔ le.

    (A) bù rán

    (B) suī rán

    (C) hū rán

    (D) dāng rán

---

52. 你打電話來的時候，我 ___ 吃飯。

    (A) 正好

    (B) 正是

    (C) 正在

    (D) 正有

52. 你打电话来的时候，我 ___ 吃饭。

    (A) 正好

    (B) 正是

    (C) 正在

    (D) 正有

52. ㄋㄧ ㄉㄚ ㄉㄧㄢ ㄏㄨㄚ ㄌㄞ ㄉㄜ ㄕ ㄏㄡ，ㄨㄛ ___ ㄔ ㄈㄢ。

    (A) ㄓㄥ ㄏㄠ

    (B) ㄓㄥ ㄕ

    (C) ㄓㄥ ㄗㄞ

    (D) ㄓㄥ ㄧㄡ

52. Nǐ dǎ diàn huà lái de shí hòu, wǒ ___ chī fàn.

    (A) zhèng hǎo

    (B) zhèng shì

    (C) zhèng zài

    (D) zhèng yǒu

---

53. 他___聽話，___還打架。

    (A) 不但不 … 而且

    (B) 雖然 … 並且

    (C) 因爲 … 所以

    (D) 只是 … 可以

53. 他___听话，___还打架。

    (A) 不但不 … 而且

    (B) 虽然 … 並且

    (C) 因为 … 所以

    (D) 只是 … 可以

53. ㄊㄚ ___ ㄊㄧㄥ ㄏㄨㄚ，___ ㄏㄞ ㄉㄚ ㄐㄧㄚ。

    (A) ㄅㄨ ㄉㄢ ㄅㄨ … ㄦ ㄑㄧㄝ

    (B) ㄙㄨㄟ ㄖㄢ … ㄅㄧㄥ ㄑㄧㄝ

    (C) ㄧㄣ ㄨㄟ … ㄙㄨㄛ ㄧ

    (D) ㄓ ㄕ … ㄎㄜ ㄧ

53. Tā ___ tīng huà, ___ hái dǎ jià.

    (A) bú dàn bù .... ér qiě

    (B) suī rán .... bìng qiě

    (C) yīn wèi .... suǒ yǐ

    (D) zhǐ shì .... kě yǐ

54. ＿＿＿ 你喜歡，＿＿買吧！不要去管價
　　 錢多貴。

    (A) 無論…都

    (B) 要是…就

    (C) 雖然…但是

    (D) 不但…而且

54. ＿＿＿ 你喜欢，＿＿买吧！不要去管价
　　 钱多贵。

    (A) 无论…都

    (B) 要是…就

    (C) 虽然…但是

    (D) 不但…而且

54. ＿＿＿ ㄋ一 ㄒ一 ㄏㄨㄢ，＿＿ㄇㄞ ㄅㄚ！ㄅㄨ ㄧㄠ ㄑㄩ ㄍㄨㄢ
　　 ㄐ一ㄚ ㄑ一ㄢ ㄉㄨㄛ ㄍㄨㄟ 。

    (A) ㄨ ㄌㄨㄣ … ㄉㄡ

    (B) ㄧㄠ ㄕ … ㄐ一ㄡ

    (C) ㄙㄨㄟ ㄖㄢ … ㄉㄢ ㄕ

    (D) ㄅㄨ ㄉㄢ … ㄦ ㄑ一ㄝ

54. ＿＿＿ nǐ xǐ huān, ＿＿ mǎi ba! Bú yào qù guǎn
　　 jià qián duó guì.

    (A) Wú lùn .... dōu

    (B) Yào shì .... jiù

    (C) Suī rán .... dàn shì

    (D) Bú dàn .... ér qiě

---

55. ＿＿＿ 你説對不起，＿＿＿他會生氣。

    (A) 除了…都

    (B) 要是…就

    (C) 除非…要不然

    (D) 不但…而且

55. ＿＿＿ 你说对不起，＿＿＿他会生气。

    (A) 除了…都

    (B) 要是…就

    (C) 除非…要不然

    (D) 不但…而且

55. ＿＿＿ ㄋ一 ㄕㄨㄛ ㄉㄨㄟ ㄅㄨ ㄑ一，＿＿＿ㄊㄚ ㄏㄨㄟ ㄕㄥ ㄑ一 。

    (A) ㄔㄨ ㄌㄜ … ㄉㄡ

    (B) ㄧㄠ ㄕ … ㄐ一ㄡ

    (C) ㄔㄨ ㄈㄟ … ㄧㄠ ㄅㄨ ㄖㄢ

    (D) ㄅㄨ ㄉㄢ … ㄦ ㄑ一ㄝ

55. ＿＿＿ nǐ shuō duì bù qǐ, ＿＿＿ tā huì shēng qì.

    (A) Chú le .... dōu

    (B) Yào shì .... jiù

    (C) Chú fēi .... yào bù rán

    (D) Bú dàn .... ér qiě

Directions: Read the following selections carefully for comprehension. Each selection is followed by one or more questions or incomplete statements based on its content. Select the answer or completion that is best according to the passage and fill in the corresponding oval on the answer sheet.

THIS SECTION OF THE TEST IS PRESENTED IN TWO WRITING SYSTEMS: TRADITIONAL CHARACTERS AND SIMPLIFIED CHARACTERS. IT IS RECOMMENDED THAT YOU CHOOSE <u>ONLY</u> THAT WRITING SYSTEM WITH WHICH YOU ARE MOST FAMILIAR AS YOU WORK THROUGH THIS SECTION OF THE TEST.

 # 56~57

泡茶時，第一泡一分鐘就可以喝了。第二泡增加十五秒，第三泡在第二泡的時間上再增加二十五秒，第四泡又在第三泡的時間上增加三十五秒。

泡茶时，第一泡一分钟就可以喝了。第二泡增加十五秒，第三泡在第二泡的时间上再增加二十五秒，第四泡又在第三泡的时间上增加三十五秒。

Question 56　　How long does it take to prepare the first round serving?

(A)　one minute

(B)　one minute and fifteen seconds

(C)　one minute and forty seconds

(D)　two minutes and fifteen seconds

Question 57　　According to the instruction, the third round serving takes _____ longer to prepare than the second round serving.

(A)　fifteen seconds

(B)　twenty five seconds

(C)　forty seconds

(D)　one minute

58

请 勿 吸 煙   请 勿 吸 烟

Question 58   What does this sign mean?

(A)   No eating

(B)   No parking

(C)   No visitors

(D)   No smoking

59

謝 絕 參 觀   谢 绝 参 观

Question 59   What does this sign mean?

(A)   No eating

(B)   No parking

(C)   No visitors

(D)   Thank you for coming

60

Question 60   What does this sign mean?

(A)   Caution: Danger

(B)   Go forward

(C)   Beware of small kids

(D)   No noise allowed

61

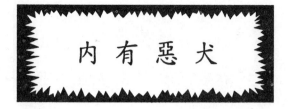 

Question 61   What does this sign mean?

(A)   No barking

(B)   Beware of dogs

(C)   Dog training inside

(D)   No mail

62~63

免費服務電話		免费服务电话	
81-2310	（長途）	81-2310	（长途）
81-2311	（市內）	81-2311	（市内）
81-2312	（北部地區）	81-2312	（北部地区）
81-2313	（南部地區）	81-2313	（南部地区）

Question 62   What is this for?

(A)   a toll-free service

(B)   an information service

(C)   an emergency service

(D)   a hot line service

Question 63   If you want to call a local service, which number should you call?

(A)   81-2310

(B)   81-2311

(C)   81-2312

(D)   81-2313

64

☎ 電話月租費用：

每月55元，租約至少五個月

☎ 电话月租费用：

每月55元，租约至少五个月

Question 64   If you want to rent it, which of the following is possible?

(A)   renting for fifty five days

(B)   renting for three months

(C)   renting for six months

(D)   none of the above

65~66

一艘客船從美國紐約開到中國上
海，不幸中途在日本附近沉沒。
船上的250位旅客，大多被救起
，卻有十位旅客不幸罹難。

一艘客船从美国纽约开到中国上
海，不幸中途在日本附近沉没。
船上的250位旅客，大多被救起
，却有十位旅客不幸罹难。

Question 65   Where did this ship start its journey from?

(A)   Japan

(B)   New York, USA

(C)   China

(D)   Shanghai

Question 66   How many passengers were drowned?

(A)   300

(B)   290

(C)   10

(D)   240

愛玲剛從德國的一所大學畢業，學的是法律，聽說要回美國發展。

愛玲刚从德国的一所大学毕业，学的是法律，听说要回美国发展。

Question 67   Which country did she get her degree from?

    (A)   USA

    (B)   China

    (C)   Germany

    (D)   Japan

Question 68   What was her major?

    (A)   law

    (B)   medicine

    (C)   accounting

    (D)   business

69

5月3日開出
14　15　36
40　41　42
獎金四百萬

5月3日开出
14　15　36
40　41　42
奖金四百万

Question 69   If you pick up all 6 of the correct numbers, how much money will you win?

    (A) $400.00

    (B) $4,000,000.00

    (C) $400,000.00

    (D) $40,000.00

70

行 人 止 步

行 人 止 步

Question 70   What does this sign mean?

(A)   No banking

(B)   No parking

(C)   Beware of small kids

(D)   No trespassing

71~73

叔叔：
　　我們到臺北已經一個星期了。臺北的風景很美，我們照了很多相片。明天我們要到臺南去看外祖父外祖母，大約十天後回美國。敬祝
　　安康！

姪 大中 敬上
八月十五日

叔叔：
　　我们到台北已经一个星期了。台北的风景很美，我们照了很多相片。明天我们要到台南去看外祖父外祖母，大约十天后回美国。敬祝
　　安康！

姪 大中 敬上
八月十五日

Question 71   The letter is addressed to

(A)   his friend

(B)   his parents

(C)   his grandparents

(D)   his uncle

Question 72   What is Da Zhong's purpose to go to Taiwan?

(A)   to visit his relatives

(B)   to visit his grandparents on his mother's side

(C)   to visit his great grandparents

(D)   to visit his friends

Question 73   When will Da Zhong go back to the United States?

(A)   around August 15

(B)   around August 22

(C)   around August 25

(D)   around the Labor Day

 # 74~77

我今年十七歲，上十一年級。我最喜歡的科目是化學，最不喜歡的科目是歷史。每個星期除了上學，我還要練琴，到市立圖書館打工，每天睡覺時間只有五個小時。

我今年十七岁，上十一年级。我最喜欢的科目是化学，最不喜欢的科目是历史。每个星期除了上学，我还要练琴，到市立图书馆打工，每天睡觉时间只有五个小时。

Question 74   What grade is the author?

(A)   Sophomore

(B)   Junior

(C)   Senior

(D)   Freshman

Question 75   What is the subject the author likes the least?

(A)   chemistry

(B)   history

(C)   music

(D)   piano

Question 76   Where does he work?

(A)   at school

(B)   at a studio

(C)   at a restaurant

(D)   at a public library

Question 77 How old is the author?

(A)   17 years old

(B)   11 years old

(C)   5 years old

(D)   12 years old

78~81

```
86.01.11 臺灣鐵路局

自強  1010次  10:11開 [孩]

臺南 → 臺北  10車45號

票價  374元

090108-026    限當日車次有效
```

```
86.01.11 台湾铁路局

自强  1010次  10:11开 [孩]

台南 → 台北  10车45号

票价  374元

090108-026    限当日车次有效
```

Question 78 What type of ticket is this?

(A)   a movie ticket

(B)   a train ticket

(C)   an airline ticket

(D)   a bus ticket

Question 79 When is the ticket valid?

(A)   Jan. 11th, 1997

(B)   Nov. 1st, 1997

(C)   Oct. 10th, 1997

(D)   Oct. 11th, 1997

Question 80 What is the destination of the trip?

(A)   Tainan

(B)   Taipei

(C)   Taichung

(D)   Taiwan

Question 81	The departing time on the ticket is

(A)	10:00

(B)	10:11

(C)	10:10

(D)	01:11

 # 82~84

早在四千多年前，希臘人已開始食用香蕉。它原產在亞洲，十五、六世紀時，傳到非洲和中南美洲。一百年前，香蕉在西歐、美國還是一種稀有的水果，直到十九世紀初，第一批香蕉才從中南美運到美國。

早在四千多年前，希腊人已开始食用香蕉。它原产在亚洲，十五、六世纪时，传到非洲和中南美洲。一百年前，香蕉在西欧、美国还是一种稀有的水果，直到十九世纪初，第一批香蕉才从中南美运到美国。

Question 82	When did the first batch of bananas arrive in the United States?

(A)	200 years ago

(B)	in the 15th century

(C)	in the 16th century

(D)	in the 19th century

Question 83	Where did the banana originate

(A)	Asia

(B)	Europe

(C)	Africa

(D)	South America

Question 84	How early did Greeks start eating bananas?

(A)	in the beginning of the 19th century

(B)	more than 4000 years ago

(C)	over 100 years ago

(D)	between the 15th and 16th century

85

故 宮 文 物　月

刊

故 宮 文 物　月

刊

Question 85　　How often is this magazine published?

(A)　weekly

(B)　monthly

(C)　bi-monthly

(D)　quarterly

SAT II 中文模擬試卷 第四套
Section I : Listening Comprehension

Part A

Directions: In this part of the test you will hear short questions, statements, or exchanges in Mandarin Chinese, follow by three responses designated (A), (B), and (C). You will hear the statements or questions, as well as the responses, just one time and they are not printed in your test booklet. Therefore, you must listen very carefully. Select the best response and fill in the corresponding oval on your answer sheet. You will have 15 seconds to answer each question.

Question 1   (A)   (B)   (C)

Question 2   (A)   (B)   (C)

Question 3   (A)   (B)   (C)

Question 4   (A)   (B)   (C)

Question 5   (A)   (B)   (C)

Question 6   (A)   (B)   (C)

Question 7   (A)   (B)   (C)

Question 8   (A)   (B)   (C)

Question 9   (A)   (B)   (C)

Question 10   (A)   (B)   (C)

Question 11   (A)   (B)   (C)

Question 12   (A)   (B)   (C)

Question 13   (A)   (B)   (C)

Question 14   (A)   (B)   (C)

Question 15   (A)   (B)   (C)

Part B

Directions: You will now hear a series of short selections. You will hear them only once and they are not printed in your test booklet. After each selection, you will be asked one or more questions about what you have just heard. These questions, with four possible answers, are printed in your test booklet. Select the best answer to each question from among the four choices given and fill in the corresponding oval on your answer sheet. You will have 15 seconds to answer each question.

16

Question 16   What type of test did Linda not do well on?

(A)   math

(B)   chemistry

(C)   P.E.

(D)   language

17~18

Question 17   Where does this conversation take place?

(A)   on the street

(B)   In the airport

(C)   at the post office

(D)   at a movie theater

Question 18   What does the man want?

(A)   to ask for directions

(B)   to mail an airmail letter

(C)   to buy some post cards

(D)   to buy an airplane ticket

19~20

Question 19   Whom is the woman looking for?

(A)   a 3 year-old girl

(B)   a 3 year-old boy

(C)   a 5 year-old girl

(D)   a 5 year-old boy

Question 20   Where does this conversation most likely take place?

(A)   shopping center

(B)   book store

(C)   hospital

(D)   supermarket

 # 21~22

Question 21   What day is this year's moon festival?

      (A)   Sunday

      (B)   Monday

      (C)   Wednesday

      (D)   Friday

Question 22   How many boxes of moon cake is the man going to purchase?

      (A)   one

      (B)   two

      (C)   three

      (D)   four

 # 23

Question 23   What's the conversation about?

      (A)   talking about a traveler

      (B)   talking about a newspaper

      (C)   talking about Earth

      (D)   talking about English

 # 24~25

Question 24   Where does this conversation most likely take place?

      (A)   post office

      (B)   book store

      (C)   supermarket

      (D)   library

Question 25   How long was the book overdue?

      (A)   one day

      (B)   two days

      (C)   three days

      (D)   four days

26~27

Question 26

What is the purpose of this conversation?

(A)   to apply for a job

(B)   to sell a Chinese book

(C)   to ask a homework question

(D)   to notify an absence

Question 27

What is the relationship between professor Zhang and the caller?

(A)   mother-son

(B)   teacher-student

(C)   employee-employer

(D)   friends

28~30

Question 28

What's the boy asking the girl?

(A)   to go with him to the movie

(B)   to go out to dinner

(C)   to go to a dance with him

(D)   to go to a concert with him

Question 29

Why can't she go with him tonight?

(A)   It's her birthday.

(B)   It's her mother's birthday.

(C)   It's her grandmother's birthday.

(D)   It's her grandfather's birthday.

Question 30

What day and time did they eventually set the date?

(A)   tomorrow at 6:00 PM

(B)   the day after tomorrow at 6:30 PM

(C)   tomorrow at 6:30 PM

(D)   the day after tomorrow at 6:00 PM

SAT II 中文模擬試題 第四套
Section I : Listening Comprehension

Part A

Directions: In this part of the test you will hear short questions, statements, or exchanges in Mandarin Chinese, followed by three responses designated (A), (B), and (C). You will hear the statements or questions, as well as the responses, just one time and they are not printed in your test booklet. Therefore, you must listen very carefully. Select the best response and fill in the corresponding oval on your answer sheet. You will have 15 seconds to answer each question.

Question 1

我把我的錢包放在這裏，不知道妳看見了沒有？

    (A) 看得見。

    (B) 看不見。

    (C) 沒看見。

Question 2

那本書好看嗎？

    (A) 有什麼意思。

    (B) 沒什麼意思。

    (C) 真不好意思。

Question 3

請問您要什麼甜點？

    (A) 我要什錦炒麵。

    (B) 我要草莓蛋糕。

    (C) 我要炸豬排。

Question 4

現在汽油貴不貴？

    (A) 在加油站加油。

    (B) 不太貴

    (C) 開車得用汽油。

Question 5

你想喝點什麼？

    (A) 夏天要多喝水。

    (B) 那還是牛奶吧！

    (C) 橘子汁。

Question 6

現在是幾點鐘？

    (A) 我家有兩個鐘

    (B) 我喜歡大鐘。

    (C) 我想是八點多了吧！

Question 7

你會燒中國菜嗎？

    (A) 我喜歡吃中國菜。

    (B) 會一點。

    (C) 中國菜很有名。

Question 8

今年夏天舊金山將有規模不小的中國古文物展覽。

    (A) 今年夏天會涼快嗎？

    (B) 真的嗎？我最喜歡中國文物了。

    (C) 我喜歡去舊金山。

Question 9

請問王先生在嗎？

    (A) 他在，請問您是哪一位？

    (B) 他在，請問您找哪一位？

    (C) 他在，請問您要哪一位？

Question 10

今天是五月五號。

    (A) 那麼明天就是五月四號。

    (B) 那麼前天就是五月四號。

    (C) 那麼昨天就是五月四號。

Question 11

這個暑假你去玩了哪些地方？

    (A) 我要去英國和法國玩。

    (B) 我會到中國和日本。

    (C) 我去了加拿大和美國。

Question 12

這場音樂會很熱門，我們得早點去買票。

　　(A) 是啊！我們趕快去買吧！

　　(B) 我的朋友也買了。

　　(C) 音樂會七點開始。

Question 13

我想買二十張37分的郵票。

　　(A) 好，請先貼郵票。

　　(B) 好，你可以用自動提款機。

　　(C) 好，一共是七元四角。

Question 14

女：我感冒頭痛，很不舒服。

男：你看醫生了嗎？

　　(A) 真的很不舒服嗎？

　　(B) 沒有，只吃了點藥。

　　(C) 溫度很高，好像發燒了。

Question 15

男：妳暑假有什麼計劃？

女：我們全家要去旅行。

男：打算上哪兒去？

　　(A) 去歐洲。

　　(B) 去旅行社。

　　(C) 去圖書館。

Part B

Directions: You will now hear a series of short selections. You will hear them <u>only once</u> and they are not printed in your test booklet. After each selection, you will be asked one or more questions about what you have just heard. These questions, with four possible answers, are printed in your test booklet. Select the best answer to each question from among the four choices given and fill in the corresponding oval on your answer sheet. You will have 15 seconds to answer each question.

Question 16

　　男：玲達，妳今天考試考得怎麼樣？

　　女：唉！別提了，有很多文法都不會。

　　男：其他的呢？

　　女：還可以。

Question 17~18

　　女：請問，寄到中國的航空信，要貼多少錢的郵票？

　　男：要是不超重，郵費是一塊二。

　　女：大概幾天可以寄到？

　　男：差不多一個星期就到了。

Question 19~20

　　女：先生，請問你有沒有看到一個五歲的小男孩？他穿著白色上
　　　　衣，藍色的褲子和一雙黑色的皮鞋。

　　男：有啊！我剛才看見他走進前面那家玩具店裏。

　　女：謝謝您，我得趕快去找他。

Question 21~22

　　男：中秋節快到了，我想買兩盒月餅請大家吃。

　　女：好啊！你知道今年的中秋節是哪一天嗎？

　　男：九月二十七日。

　　女：星期幾？

　　男：星期五。

Question 23

男：你看報了嗎？英國旅行家徒步旅行，繞地球一週。

女：這新聞我看了，他真有兩下子。

Question 24~25

男：張太太，妳也來借書啊？

女：我來還書的，這本書前天就到期了，最近太忙了，沒時間來還。

Question 26~27

男：喂，請問張教授在嗎？

女：他剛出去，請問你有什麼事？

男：我是他的學生，這個星期六，我有個辯論比賽，不能去上中文課，麻煩您轉告張教授，好嗎？

女：沒問題，等他回來，我會轉告他。

Question 28~30

男：今晚我們去看電影怎麼樣？

女：沒辦法，今天是奶奶的生日，晚上我們全家要一起出去吃飯。明天晚上我沒事，明天去看好嗎？

男：好，一言為定，我六點半去接妳。

Directions: This section consists of a number of incomplete statements, each of which has four suggested completions. Select the word or phrase that best completes the sentence structurally and logically. Please fill in the corresponding oval on the answer sheet.
THE QUESTIONS ARE PRESENTED IN FOUR DIFFERENT WRITING SYSTEMS: TRADITIONAL CHARACTERS, SIMPLIFIED CHARACTERS, PINYIN ROMANIZATION, AND CHINESE PHONETIC ALPHABET(BO PO MO FO). TO SAVE TIME, IT IS RECOMMENDED THAT YOU CHOOSE THE WRITING SYSTEM WITH WHICH YOU ARE MOST FAMILIAR WITH AND **READ ONLY THAT VERSION OF THE QUESTION.**

31. 現在的流行歌曲 ＿＿＿好聽，＿＿有些音樂家認爲它們不夠正統。

    (A) 不但…而且

    (B) 雖然…但是

    (C) 如果…就會

    (D) 因爲…所以

31. 現在的流行歌曲 ＿＿＿好听，＿＿有些音乐家认为它们不够正统。

    (A) 不但…而且

    (B) 虽然…但是

    (C) 如果…就会

    (D) 因为…所以

31. ㄒㄧㄢˋㄗㄞˋㄉㄜ˙ㄌㄧㄡˊㄒㄧㄥˊㄍㄜㄑㄩˇ ＿＿＿ㄏㄠˇㄊㄧㄥ，＿＿ㄧㄡˇㄒㄧㄝㄧㄣㄩㄝˋㄐㄧㄚㄖㄣˋㄨㄟˊㄊㄚㄇㄣ˙ㄅㄨˊㄍㄡˋㄓㄥˋㄊㄨㄥˇ。

    (A) ㄅㄨˊㄉㄢˋ … ㄦˊㄑㄧㄝˇ

    (B) ㄙㄨㄟㄖㄢˊ … ㄉㄢˋㄕˋ

    (C) ㄖㄨˊㄍㄨㄛˇ … ㄐㄧㄡˋㄏㄨㄟˋ

    (D) ㄧㄣㄨㄟˋ … ㄙㄨㄛˇㄧˇ

31. Xiàn zài de liú xíng gē qǔ ＿＿ hǎo tīng, ＿＿yǒu xiē yīn yuè jiā rèn wéi tā men bú gòu zhèng tǒng.

    (A) bú dàn .... ér qiě

    (B) suī rán .... dàn shì

    (C) rú guǒ .... jiù huì

    (D) yīn wèi .... suǒ yǐ

---

32. 他不但幫我把碗筷都洗了，＿＿廚房的廚具都擦得亮亮的。

    (A) 連

    (B) 就

    (C) 才

    (D) 還

32. 他不但帮我把碗筷都洗了，＿＿厨房的厨具都擦得亮亮的。

    (A) 连

    (B) 就

    (C) 才

    (D) 还

32. ㄊㄚㄅㄨˊㄉㄢˋㄅㄤㄨㄛˇㄅㄚˇㄨㄢˇㄎㄨㄞˋㄉㄡㄒㄧˇㄌㄜ˙，＿＿ㄔㄨˊㄈㄤˊㄉㄜ˙ㄔㄨˊㄐㄩˋㄉㄡㄘㄚㄉㄜ˙ㄌㄧㄤˋㄌㄧㄤㄉㄜ˙。

    (A) ㄌㄧㄢˊ

    (B) ㄐㄧㄡˋ

    (C) ㄘㄞˊ

    (D) ㄏㄞˊ

32. Tā bú dàn bāng wǒ bǎ wǎn kuài dōu xǐ le, ＿＿ chú fáng de chú jù dōu cā de liàng liang de.

    (A) lián

    (B) jiù

    (C) cái

    (D) hái

33. 這 ＿＿＿ 鏡子擦得好亮！

    (A) 幅

    (B) 面

    (C) 座

    (D) 個

33. 这 ＿＿＿ 镜子擦得好亮！

    (A) 幅

    (B) 面

    (C) 座

    (D) 个

33. ㄓㄜ ＿＿＿ ㄐㄧㄥ˙ㄗ ㄘㄚ ㄉㄜ˙ ㄏㄠˇ ㄌㄧㄤˋ！

    (A) ㄈㄨˊ

    (B) ㄇㄧㄢˋ

    (C) ㄗㄨㄛˋ

    (D) ㄍㄜ˙

33. Zhè ＿＿＿ jìng zi cā de hǎo liàng!

    (A) fú

    (B) miàn

    (C) zuò

    (D) ge

---

34. 李大友來美國以後 ＿＿＿ 住在加州。

    (A) 不停

    (B) 一直

    (C) 不斷

    (D) 一連

34. 李大友来美国以后 ＿＿＿ 住在加州。

    (A) 不停

    (B) 一直

    (C) 不断

    (D) 一连

34. ㄌㄧˇㄉㄚˋㄧㄡˇ ㄌㄞˊ ㄇㄟˇㄍㄨㄛˊ ㄧˇㄏㄡˋ ＿＿＿ ㄓㄨˋㄗㄞˋㄐㄧㄚㄓㄡ。

    (A) ㄅㄨˋ ㄊㄧㄥˊ

    (B) ㄧˋ ㄓˊ

    (C) ㄅㄨˊ ㄉㄨㄢˋ

    (D) ㄧˋ ㄌㄧㄢˊ

34. Lǐdàyǒu lái Měiguó yǐ hòu, ＿＿＿ zhù zài Jiāzhōu.

    (A) bù tíng

    (B) yì zhí

    (C) bú duàn

    (D) yì lián

---

35. ＿＿＿ 我多練習，我 ＿＿＿ 可以做得和她一樣好。

    (A) 不管…也不

    (B) 如果…雖然

    (C) 如果…也

    (D) 因為…是

35. ＿＿＿ 我多练习，我 ＿＿＿ 可以做得和她一样好。

    (A) 不管…也不

    (B) 如果…虽然

    (C) 如果…也

    (D) 因为…是

35. ＿＿＿ ㄨㄛˇ ㄉㄨㄛ ㄌㄧㄢˋㄒㄧˊ，ㄨㄛˇ ＿＿＿ ㄎㄜˇ ㄧˇ ㄗㄨㄛˋ ㄉㄜ˙ ㄏㄢˋ ㄊㄚ ㄧˊ ㄧㄤˋ ㄏㄠˇ。

    (A) ㄅㄨˋ ㄍㄨㄢˇ … ㄧㄝˇ ㄅㄨˋ

    (B) ㄖㄨˊ ㄍㄨㄛˇ … ㄙㄨㄟ ㄖㄢˊ

    (C) ㄖㄨˊ ㄍㄨㄛˇ … ㄧㄝˇ

    (D) ㄧㄣ ㄨㄟˋ … ㄕˋ

35. ＿＿＿ wǒ duō liàn xí, wǒ ＿＿＿ kě yǐ zuò de hàn tā yí yàng hǎo.

    (A) Bù guǎn .... yě bù

    (B) Rú guǒ .... suī rán

    (C) Rú guǒ.... yě

    (D) Yīn wèi .... shì

36.妹妹是家裏____不愛打球的人。

(A) 唯一

(B) 不只

(C) 所有

(D) 只有

36.ㄇㄟˋㄇㄟ˙ㄕˋㄐㄧㄚㄌㄧˇ____ㄅㄨˊㄞˋㄉㄚˇㄑㄧㄡˊ˙ㄉㄜㄖㄣˊ。

(A) ㄨㄟˊㄧ

(B) ㄅㄨˋㄓˇ

(C) ㄙㄨㄛˇㄧㄡˇ

(D) ㄓˇㄧㄡˇ

36.妹妹是家里____不爱打球的人。

(A) 唯一

(B) 不只

(C) 所有

(D) 只有

36. Mèi mei shì jiā lǐ ____ bú ài dǎ qiú de rén.

(A) wéi yī

(B) bù zhǐ

(C) suǒ yǒu

(D) zhǐ yǒu

---

37. 別人都懂了，____我還不懂。

(A) 只有

(B) 爲了

(C) 真是

(D) 什麼

37.ㄅㄧㄝˊㄖㄣˊㄉㄡㄉㄨㄥˇ˙ㄌㄜ，____ㄨㄛˇㄏㄞˊㄅㄨˋㄉㄨㄥˇ。

(A) ㄓˇㄧㄡˇ

(B) ㄨㄟˋ˙ㄌㄜ

(C) ㄓㄣ˙ㄕˋ

(D) ㄕㄣˊ˙ㄇㄜ

37. 别人都懂了，____我还不懂。

(A) 只有

(B) 为了

(C) 真是

(D) 什么

37. Bié rén dōu dǒng le, ____ wǒ hái bù dǒng.

(A) zhǐ yǒu

(B) wèi le

(C) zhēn shì

(D) shén me

---

38. 奶奶、姐姐剛旅行____需要休息兩天。

(A) 起來

(B) 進去

(C) 回來

(D) 上去

38.ㄋㄞˇ˙ㄋㄞ、ㄐㄧㄝˇ˙ㄐㄧㄝㄍㄤㄌㄩˇㄒㄧㄥˊ____ㄒㄩㄧㄠˋㄒㄧㄡㄒㄧˊㄌㄧㄤˇㄊㄧㄢ。

(A) ㄑㄧˇㄌㄞˊ

(B) ㄐㄧㄣˋㄑㄩˋ

(C) ㄏㄨㄟˊㄌㄞˊ

(D) ㄕㄤˋㄑㄩˋ

38. 奶奶、姐姐刚旅行____需要休息两天。

(A) 起来

(B) 进去

(C) 回来

(D) 上去

38. Nǎi nai, jiě jie gāng lǚ xíng ____ xū yào xiū xí liǎng tiān.

(A) qǐ lái

(B) jìn qù

(C) huí lái

(D) shàng qù

39. 小李打電話來，＿＿＿＿＿＿＿。

    (A) 說他不來了今天。

    (B) 今天說他不來了。

    (C) 說他今天不來了。

    (D) 不來了說他今天。

39. 小李打电话来，＿＿＿＿＿＿＿。

    (A) 说他不来了今天。

    (B) 今天说他不来了。

    (C) 说他今天不来了。

    (D) 不来了说他今天。

39. ㄒㄠ ㄌ一 ㄉㄚ ㄉㄧㄢ ㄏㄨㄚ ㄌㄞ，＿＿＿＿＿＿＿。

    (A) ㄕㄨㄛ ㄊㄚ ㄅㄨ ㄌㄞ ㄌㄜ ㄐㄧㄣ ㄊㄧㄢ。

    (B) ㄐㄧㄣ ㄊㄧㄢ ㄕㄨㄛ ㄊㄚ ㄅㄨ ㄌㄞ ㄌㄜ。

    (C) ㄕㄨㄛ ㄊㄚ ㄐㄧㄣ ㄊㄧㄢ ㄅㄨ ㄌㄞ ㄌㄜ。

    (D) ㄅㄨ ㄌㄞ ㄌㄜ ㄕㄨㄛ ㄊㄚ ㄐㄧㄣ ㄊㄧㄢ。

39. Xiǎolǐ dǎ diàn huà lái, ＿＿＿＿＿ .

    (A) shuō tā bù lái le jīn tiān

    (B) jīn tiān shuō tā bù lái le

    (C) shuō tā jīn tiān bù lái le

    (D) bù lái le shuō tā jīn tiān

---

40. 她 ＿＿＿ 這部電影的故事感動了。

    (A) 把

    (B) 跟

    (C) 被

    (D) 和

40. 她 ＿＿＿ 这部电影的故事感动了。

    (A) 把

    (B) 跟

    (C) 被

    (D) 和

40. ㄊㄚ ＿＿＿ ㄓㄜ ㄅㄨ ㄉㄧㄢ ㄧㄥ ㄉㄜ ㄍㄨ ㄕ ㄍㄢ ㄉㄨㄥ ㄌㄜ。

    (A) ㄅㄚ

    (B) ㄍㄣ

    (C) ㄅㄟ

    (D) ㄏㄢ

40. Tā ＿＿＿ zhè bù diàn yǐng de gù shì gǎn dòng le.

    (A) bǎ

    (B) gēn

    (C) bèi

    (D) hàn

---

41. 他總是 ＿＿＿ 家裏打掃得乾乾淨淨。

    (A) 在

    (B) 被

    (C) 拿

    (D) 把

41. 他总是 ＿＿＿ 家里打扫得干干净净。

    (A) 在

    (B) 被

    (C) 拿

    (D) 把

41. ㄊㄚ ㄗㄨㄥ ㄕ ＿＿＿ ㄐㄧㄚ ㄌㄧ ㄉㄚ ㄙㄠ ㄉㄜ ㄍㄢ ㄍㄢ ㄐㄧㄥ ㄐㄧㄥ。

    (A) ㄗㄞ

    (B) ㄅㄟ

    (C) ㄋㄚ

    (D) ㄅㄚ

41. Tā zǒng shì ＿＿＿ jiā lǐ dǎ sǎo de gān gān jìng jing.

    (A) zài

    (B) bèi

    (C) ná

    (D) bǎ

42. 我 ____ 吃過飯了。

    (A) 已經

    (B) 正在

    (C) 不在

    (D) 沒有

42. ㄨㄛˇ ____ ㄔ ㄍㄨㄛˋ ㄈㄢˋ ㄌㄜ。

    (A) ㄧˇ ㄐㄧㄥ

    (B) ㄓㄥˋ ㄗㄞˋ

    (C) ㄅㄨˊ ㄗㄞˋ

    (D) ㄇㄟˊ ㄧㄡˇ

42. 我 ____ 吃过饭了。

    (A) 已经

    (B) 正在

    (C) 不在

    (D) 没有

42. Wǒ ____ chī guò fàn le.

    (A) yǐ jīng

    (B) zhèng zài

    (C) bú zài

    (D) méi yǒu

---

43. 你喜歡吃中餐____喜歡吃西餐？

    (A) 又是

    (B) 可是

    (C) 還是

    (D) 也是

43. ㄋㄧˇ ㄒㄧ ㄏㄨㄢ ㄔ ㄓㄨㄥ ㄘㄢ ____ ㄒㄧ ㄏㄨㄢ ㄔ ㄒㄧ ㄘㄢ？

    (A) ㄧㄡˋ ㄕˋ

    (B) ㄎㄜˇ ㄕˋ

    (C) ㄏㄞˊ ㄕˋ

    (D) ㄧㄝˇ ㄕˋ

43. 你喜欢吃中餐____喜欢吃西餐？

    (A) 又是

    (B) 可是

    (C) 还是

    (D) 也是

43. Nǐ xǐ huān chī zhōng cān ____ xǐ huān chī xī cān?

    (A) yòu shì

    (B) kě shì

    (C) hái shì

    (D) yě shì

---

44. 考試八點半就開始了，你怎麼現在 ____ 來？

    (A) 才

    (B) 就

    (C) 再

    (D) 不

44. ㄎㄠˇ ㄕˋ ㄅㄚ ㄉㄧㄢˇ ㄅㄢˋ ㄐㄧㄡˋ ㄎㄞ ㄕˇ ㄌㄜ，ㄋㄧˇ ㄗㄣˇ ㄇㄜ ㄒㄧㄢˋ ㄗㄞˋ ____ ㄌㄞˊ？

    (A) ㄘㄞˊ

    (B) ㄐㄧㄡˋ

    (C) ㄗㄞˋ

    (D) ㄅㄨˋ

44. 考试八点半就开始了，你怎么现在 ____ 来？

    (A) 才

    (B) 就

    (C) 再

    (D) 不

44. Kǎo shì bā diǎn bàn jiù kāi shǐ le, nǐ zěn me xiàn zài ____ lái?

    (A) cái

    (B) jiù

    (C) zài

    (D) bù

45. 胡老師，真對不起，我沒聽清楚，
   請您 ___ 說一次。
   (A) 才
   (B) 還
   (C) 就
   (D) 再

45. ㄏㄨˊ ㄌㄠˇ ㄕ，ㄓㄣ ㄉㄨㄟˋ ㄅㄨˋ ㄑㄧˇ，ㄨㄛˇ ㄇㄟˊ ㄊㄧㄥ ㄑㄧㄥ ㄔㄨˇ，
   ㄑㄧㄥˇ ㄋㄧㄣˊ ___ ㄕㄨㄛ ㄧˊ ㄘˋ。
   (A) ㄘㄞˊ
   (B) ㄏㄞˊ
   (C) ㄐㄧㄡˋ
   (D) ㄗㄞˋ

45. 胡老师，真对不起，我没听清楚，
   请您 ___ 说一次。
   (A) 才
   (B) 还
   (C) 就
   (D) 再

45. Hú lǎo shī, zhēn duì bù qǐ, wǒ méi tīng qīng chǔ, qǐng nín ___ shuō yí cì.
   (A) cái
   (B) hái
   (C) jiù
   (D) zài

---

46. 上了一天的課，_____。
   (A) 我覺得一點累。
   (B) 我覺得累一點。
   (C) 我覺得累很多。
   (D) 我覺得有一點兒累。

46. ㄕㄤˋ ㄌㄜ ㄧ ㄊㄧㄢ ㄉㄜ ㄎㄜˋ，_____。
   (A) ㄨㄛˇ ㄐㄩㄝˊ ㄉㄜ ㄧ ㄉㄧㄢˇ ㄌㄟˋ。
   (B) ㄨㄛˇ ㄐㄩㄝˊ ㄉㄜ ㄌㄟˋ ㄧ ㄉㄧㄢˇ。
   (C) ㄨㄛˇ ㄐㄩㄝˊ ㄉㄜ ㄌㄟˋ ㄏㄣˇ ㄉㄨㄛ。
   (D) ㄨㄛˇ ㄐㄩㄝˊ ㄉㄜ ㄧㄡˇ ㄧ ㄉㄧㄢˇ ㄦ ㄌㄟˋ。

46. 上了一天的课，_____。
   (A) 我觉得一点累。
   (B) 我觉得累一点。
   (C) 我觉得累很多。
   (D) 我觉得有一点儿累。

46. Shàng le yì tiān de kè, _____.
   (A) wǒ jué de yì diǎn lèi
   (B) wǒ jué de lèi yì diǎn
   (C) wǒ jué de lèi hěn duō
   (D) wǒ jué de yǒu yì diǎnr lèi

---

47. 請問我把錢還給你了 ___？
   (A) 呢
   (B) 嗎
   (C) 哇
   (D) 呀

47. ㄑㄧㄥˇ ㄨㄣˋ ㄨㄛˇ ㄅㄚˇ ㄑㄧㄢˊ ㄏㄨㄢˊ ㄍㄟˇ ㄋㄧˇ ㄌㄜ ___？
   (A) ㄋㄜ
   (B) ㄇㄚ
   (C) ㄨㄚ
   (D) ㄧㄚ

47. 请问我把钱还给你了 ___？
   (A) 呢
   (B) 吗
   (C) 哇
   (D) 呀

47. Qǐng wèn wǒ bǎ qián huán gěi nǐ le ___？
   (A) na
   (B) ma
   (C) wa
   (D) ya

48. 他只＿＿了三分鐘，就想出答案。

    (A) 猜

    (B) 花

    (C) 才

    (D) 就

48. 他只＿＿了三分钟，就想出答案。

    (A) 猜

    (B) 花

    (C) 才

    (D) 就

48. (Zhuyin)

    (A)

    (B)

    (C)

    (D)

48. Tā zhǐ ＿＿＿le sān fēn zhōng, jiù xiǎng chū dá àn.

    (A) cāi

    (B) huā

    (C) cái

    (D) jiù

---

49. 王大中＿＿聰明＿＿也很用功。

    (A) 不但…而且

    (B) 因為…所以

    (C) 如果…就要

    (D) 雖然…但是

49. 王大中＿＿聪明＿＿也很用功。

    (A) 不但…而且

    (B) 因为…所以

    (C) 如果…就要

    (D) 虽然…但是

49. (Zhuyin)

    (A)

    (B)

    (C)

    (D)

49. Wángdàzhōng ＿＿ cōng míng ＿＿ yě hěn yòng gōng.

    (A) bú dàn ... ér qiě

    (B) yīn wèi ... suǒ yǐ

    (C) rú guǒ ... jiù yào

    (D) suī rán ... dàn shì

---

50. 我很想去看電影，＿＿爸爸不答應。

    (A) 也是

    (B) 真是

    (C) 又是

    (D) 可是

50. 我很想去看电影，＿＿爸爸不答应。

    (A) 也是

    (B) 真是

    (C) 又是

    (D) 可是

50. (Zhuyin)

    (A)

    (B)

    (C)

    (D)

50. Wǒ hěn xiǎng qù kàn diàn yǐng, ＿＿ bà ba bù dā yìng.

    (A) yě shì

    (B) zhēn shì

    (C) yòu shì

    (D) kě shì

51. _____ 她怎麼説，___ 無法改變爸爸的看法。

    (A) 除了…還要

    (B) 雖然…但是

    (C) 無論…都

    (D) 如果…就要

51. _____ 她怎么说，___ 无法改变爸爸的看法。

    (A) 除了…还要

    (B) 虽然…但是

    (C) 无论…都

    (D) 如果…就要

51. _____ tā zěn me shuō, ___ wú fǎ gǎi biàn bà ba de kàn fǎ.

    (A) Chú le .... hái yào

    (B) Suī rán .... dàn shì

    (C) Wú lùn .... dōu

    (D) Rú guǒ .... jiù yào

---

52. 他___有空___上網玩電動遊戲。

    (A) 這…都

    (B) 從 …到

    (C) 一 …就

    (D) 先 …再

52. 他___有空___上网玩电动游戏。

    (A) 这…都

    (B) 从 …到

    (C) 一 …就

    (D) 先 …再

52. Tā ___ yǒu kòng ___ shàng wǎng wán diàn dòng yóu xì.

    (A) zhè .... dōu

    (B) cóng .... dào

    (C) yì .... jiù

    (D) xiān.... zài

---

53. 請你給我一___冰水，好嗎？

    (A) 枝

    (B) 片

    (C) 杯

    (D) 個

53. 请你给我一___冰水，好吗？

    (A) 枝

    (B) 片

    (C) 杯

    (D) 个

53. Qǐng nǐ gěi wǒ yì ___ bīng shuǐ, hǎo ma?

    (A) zhī

    (B) piàn

    (C) bēi

    (D) ge

54. 我 ＿＿＿ 哥哥今天沒有來，＿＿＿ 他早就到了。

    (A) 不但…而且
    (B) 雖然…但是
    (C) 除了…以外
    (D) 以為…其實

54. ㄨㄛˇ ＿＿＿ ㄍㄜ ㄍㄜ ㄐㄧㄣ ㄊㄧㄢ ㄇㄟˊ ㄧㄡˇ ㄌㄞˊ，＿＿＿ ㄊㄚ ㄗㄠˇ ㄐㄧㄡˋ ㄉㄠˋ ㄌㄜ。

    (A) ㄅㄨˊ ㄉㄢˋ … ㄦˊ ㄑㄧㄝˇ
    (B) ㄙㄨㄟ ㄖㄢˊ … ㄉㄢˋ ㄕˋ
    (C) ㄔㄨˊ ㄌㄜ … ㄧˇ ㄨㄞˋ
    (D) ㄧˇ ㄨㄟˊ … ㄑㄧˊ ㄕˊ

55. ＿＿＿ 大家都同意了，＿＿＿ 去做吧！

    (A) 雖然…但是
    (B) 既然…就
    (C) 不但…而且
    (D) 除了…就

55. ＿＿＿ ㄉㄚˋ ㄐㄧㄚ ㄉㄡ ㄊㄨㄥˊ ㄧˋ ㄌㄜ，＿＿＿ ㄑㄩˋ ㄗㄨㄛˋ ㄅㄚ！

    (A) ㄙㄨㄟ ㄖㄢˊ … ㄉㄢˋ ㄕˋ
    (B) ㄐㄧˋ ㄖㄢˊ … ㄐㄧㄡˋ
    (C) ㄅㄨˊ ㄉㄢˋ … ㄦˊ ㄑㄧㄝˇ
    (D) ㄔㄨˊ ㄌㄜ … ㄐㄧㄡˋ

54. 我 ＿＿＿ 哥哥今天沒有來，＿＿＿ 他早就到了。

    (A) 不但…而且
    (B) 虽然…但是
    (C) 除了…以外
    (D) 以为…其实

54. Wǒ ＿＿＿ gē ge jīn tiān méi yǒu lái, ＿＿＿ tā zǎo jiù dào le.

    (A) bú dàn .... ér qiě
    (B) suī rán .... dàn shì
    (C) chú le .... yǐ wài
    (D) yǐ wéi .... qí shí

55. ＿＿＿ 大家都同意了，＿＿＿ 去做吧！

    (A) 虽然…但是
    (B) 既然…就
    (C) 不但…而且
    (D) 除了…就

55. ＿＿＿ dà jiā dōu tóng yì le, ＿＿＿ qù zuò ba!

    (A) Suī rán .... dàn shì
    (B) Jì rán .... jiù
    (C) Bú dàn .... ér qiě
    (D) Chú le .... jiù

SAT II 中文模擬試題 第四套
Section III : Reading Comprehension

Directions: Read the following selections carefully for comprehension. Each selection is followed by one or more questions or incomplete statements based on its content. Select the answer or completion that is best according to the passage and fill in the corresponding oval on the answer sheet.

THIS SECTION OF THE TEST IS PRESENTED IN TWO WRITING SYSTEMS: TRADITIONAL CHARACTERS AND SIMPLIFIED CHARACTERS. IT IS RECOMMENDED THAT YOU CHOOSE <u>ONLY</u> THAT WRITING SYSTEM WITH WHICH YOU ARE MOST FAMILIAR AS YOU WORK THROUGH THIS SECTION OF THE TEST.

 # 56~57

美國人正以驚人的速度排斥吸煙的習慣，而這也是一項全球性的趨勢。美國人的吸煙量，二十年來下降了百分之四十二，全球則降低了百分之十一。

但窮國與若干國家的青少年和年輕婦女吸煙的現象，卻有日增的跡象。全球各地歸因於吸煙的死亡案例也仍在增加。

美国人正以惊人的速度排斥吸烟的习惯，而这也是一项全球性的趋势。美国人的吸烟量，二十年来下降了百分之四十二，全球则降低了百分之十一。

但穷国与若干国家的青少年和年轻妇女吸烟的现象，却有日增的迹象。全球各地归因于吸烟的死亡案例也仍在增加。

Question 56   The amount of cigarette consumption in the world

(A)   decreased 42%

(B)   decreased 11%

(C)   increased 42%

(D)   increased 11%

Question 57   Which of the following statements is correct?

(A)   The percentage of young people smoking has decreased.

(B)   There are more Americans smoking than 20 years ago.

(C)   The smoking rate in the poor countries has decreased.

(D)   Smoking can cause death.

媽媽說，在臺灣八月八日是父親節，因為「八八」和「爸爸」音近的關係吧！

去年八月八日，我和弟弟妹妹一起送給爸爸一份禮物，直到今天，他還念念不忘，常常向朋友提起，而且言語之間充滿了驕傲和喜悅的神情。

那次我們合作畫了一張卡片，告訴爸爸他是全天下最好的爸爸。媽媽準備了早餐，讓爸爸在床上吃，我彈琴，弟弟妹妹唱歌給他聽，連小狗都加入我們的表演，一家人過了一個愉快且難忘的父親節。

妈妈说，在台湾八月八日是父亲节，因为「八八」和「爸爸」音近的关系吧！

去年八月八日，我和弟弟妹妹一起送给爸爸一分礼物，直到今天，他还念念不忘，常常向朋友提起，而且言语之间充满了骄傲和喜悦的神情。

那次我们合作画了一张卡片，告诉爸爸他是全天下最好的爸爸。妈妈准备了早餐，让爸爸在床上吃，我弹琴，弟弟妹妹唱歌给他听，连小狗都加入我们的表演，一家人过了一个愉快且难忘的父亲节。

Question 58   Based on this short essay how many people are in the family?

(A)   four

(B)   five

(C)   six

(D)   seven

Question 59   What kind of pet does this family have?

(A)   bird

(B)   cat

(C)   dog

(D)   fish

Question 60   What was the occasion?

(A)   Father's birthday

(B)   Mother's birthday

(C)   Father's day

(D)   Mother's day

61

橘子汁每瓶3元，買一送一

桔子汁每瓶3元，买一送一

Question 61　　　How much do you need to pay for 2 bottles of orange juice?

- (A)　$ 6.00
- (B)　$12.00
- (C)　$ 3.00
- (D)　$ 1.50

62~64

中國語言文化夏令營
年齡：14-20歲
北京：7月16日至8月13日
上海：7月9日至8月6日
廣州：6月25日至7月23日
報名截止日期：5月20日

中国语言文化夏令营
年龄：14-20岁
北京：7月16日至8月13日
上海：7月9日至8月6日
广州：6月25日至7月23日
报名截止日期：5月20日

Question 62　　　What is this ad for?

- (A)　a summer camp
- (B)　a tour
- (C)　a contest
- (D)　a computer show

Question 63　　　What is the deadline for registration?

- (A)　5月20日
- (B)　6月25日
- (C)　8月6日
- (D)　8月13日

Question 64   Which city is not included in this ad?

  (A)   Beijing

  (B)   Shanghai

  (C)   Guangzhou

  (D)   Hangzhou

65

美國銀行

服務時間：

星期一至星期五：

上午九點至下午四點

星期六：

上午十點至下午二點

美国银行

服务时间：

星期一至星期五：

上午九点至下午四点

星期六：

上午十点至下午二点

Question 65   What time does the bank close on Wednesdays?

  (A)   9:00 pm

  (B)   2:00 pm

  (C)   4:00 pm

  (D)   10:00 pm

66

Question 66   What does this sign mean?

  (A)   Itinerary

  (B)   Program

  (C)   Holiday Schedule

  (D)   Flight Schedule

67

失物招领　　　　　　　失物招领

Question 67　　What does this sign mean?

(A)　　No Visitor

(B)　　Financial Aid

(C)　　Lost & Found

(D)　　Registrar

68

Question 68　　Where most likely will you see this sign?

(A)　　in a building

(B)　　on the street

(C)　　in a factory

(D)　　in a school

69

回收资源　　　　　　　回收资源

Question 69　　What does this sign mean?

(A)　　Recycle Metal & Paper Products

(B)　　Collect Old Things

(C)　　Clean Out the Garage

(D)　　Buy Kitchen Products

 # 70

已經兩點半了，你怎麼現在才吃午飯？

已经两点半了，你怎么现在才吃午饭？

Question 70 What does this question imply?

(A) It is time to eat lunch.

(B) You are late for lunch.

(C) Let's go out to eat.

(D) You shouldn't eat lunch.

 # 71~72

中華民族的歷史很悠久，約五千年左右。中國古代的四大發明：指南針、造紙、印刷和火藥，對人類文明有很大的貢獻。

中华民族的历史很悠久，约五千年左右。中国古代的四大发明：指南针、造纸、印刷和火药，对人类文明有很大的贡献。

Question 71 According to the article, how long is the history of China?

(A) 40,000 years

(B) 50,000 years

(C) 4,000 years

(D) 5,000 years

Question 72 One of the "Four Inventions" of ancient China was

(A) Traditional Chinese Medicine

(B) The Bow & Arrow

(C) The Computer

(D) Gunpowder

北京是觀光勝地，值得去的地方很多。有一句話—〝不到長城非好漢〞，因此到北京的第二天，我就迫不及待地和哥哥一家人去遊覽了世界聞名的萬里長城。

北京是观光胜地，值得去的地方很多。有一句话—〝不到长城非好汉〞，因此到北京的第二天，我就迫不及待地和哥哥一家人去游览了世界闻名的万里长城。

Question 73   Where did this person visit?

(A)   Forbidden City

(B)   Temple of Heaven

(C)   Great Wall

(D)   Imperial Palace

Question 74   With whom did this person travel?

(A)   sister

(B)   sister's family

(C)   brother

(D)   brother's family

75

長江又名揚子江，是中國最長的河流，全長三千一百英里，僅次於南美洲的亞馬遜河，和排名第一的非洲尼羅河。

长江又名扬子江，是中国最长的河流，全长三千一百英里，仅次於南美洲的亚马逊河，和排名第一的非洲尼罗河。

Question 75   Which of the following statements is correct?

(A)   The Amazon ranks 1st in length in the world.

(B)   The source of the Nile is in Asia.

(C)   The Yangtze River is the longest river in China.

(D)   South America does not have any rivers.

 # 76

吃飯的時候，母親三番兩次地
站起來幫忙上菜、收盤子。

吃饭的时候，母亲三番两次地
站起来帮忙上菜、收盘子。

Question 76   How many times did the mother stand up?

    (A)   twice

    (B)   three times

    (C)   five times

    (D)   many times

 # 77

Question 77   What does this sign mean?

    (A)   Garage Sale

    (B)   Auction

    (C)   Big Sale

    (D)   Lower Interest Rate

 # 78

Question 78   What does this sign mean?

    (A)   Satisfaction Guaranteed

    (B)   Guest Welcome

    (C)   Vacancy

    (D)   Seats Sold Out

公寓出租

兩房一廳，安靜，交通方便

近超級市場，月租八百

晚九點後請電

(408) 574-2666

公寓出租

两房一厅，安静，交通方便

近超级市场，月租八百

晚九点后请电

(408) 574-2666

Question 79   What is this ad for?

(A)   renting an apartment

(B)   renting a house

(C)   selling an apartment

(D)   selling a house

Question 80   What is not mentioned in this ad?

(A)   It is close to a supermarket.

(B)   Rent is $800 per month.

(C)   It is a quiet place.

(D)   It is close to a library.

81

晶晶兒童合唱團
新生班
指定曲：
1. 魚兒水中游
2. 西風的話
3. 送別

晶晶儿童合唱团
新生班
指定曲：
1. 鱼儿水中游
2. 西风的话
3. 送别

Question 81   What kind of group is this?

(A)   an acting troupe

(B)   a skating club

(C)   a choir

(D)   an opera company

 # 82

瑪莉：

　　　媽媽有事出去一下，三點一刻記得去接弟弟回家。

　　　　　　　　　　媽媽留

瑪莉：

　　　妈妈有事出去一下，三点一刻记得去接弟弟回家。

　　　　　　　　　　妈妈留

Question 82　　Who will take the little brother home today?

(A)　　Mary

(B)　　mom

(C)　　dad

(D)　　friend

Question 83　　〝三點一刻〞in this note means

(A)　　3:10 pm

(B)　　3:15 pm

(C)　　3:30 pm

(D)　　3:45 pm

 # 84

男：小姐，請問這幅畫多少錢？

女：那是非賣品。

男：小姐，请问这幅画多少钱？

女：那是非卖品。

Question 84　　What does the lady mean?

(A)　　The picture is very expensive.

(B)　　It's not for sale.

(C)　　It's not mine.

(D)　　The picture is very cheap.

85

蔬果是21世紀的天然維他命，可防30種癌症。每天食用5種蔬果，可遠離癌症。

蔬果是21世纪的天然维他命，可防30种癌症。每天食用5种蔬果，可远离癌症。

Question 85   Which of the following is NOT correct according to this paragraph?

(A)   Vegetables and fruits have plenty of vitamins.

(B)   Eating more fruits could prevent cancer.

(C)   Eating 5 kinds of fruits and vegetables each day could prevent cancer.

(D)   There are 30 vitamins that could prevent cancer.

SAT II中文模擬試卷 第五套
Section I : Listening Comprehension

Part A

Directions: In this part of the test you will hear short questions, statements, or exchanges in Mandarin Chinese, follow by three responses designated (A), (B), and (C). You will hear the statements or questions, as well as the responses, just one time and they are not printed in your test booklet. Therefore, you must listen very carefully. Select the best response and fill in the corresponding oval on your answer sheet. You will have 15 seconds to answer each question.

Question 1　　(A)　　(B)　　(C)

Question 2　　(A)　　(B)　　(C)

Question 3　　(A)　　(B)　　(C)

Question 4　　(A)　　(B)　　(C)

Question 5　　(A)　　(B)　　(C)

Question 6　　(A)　　(B)　　(C)

Question 7　　(A)　　(B)　　(C)

Question 8　　(A)　　(B)　　(C)

Question 9　　(A)　　(B)　　(C)

Question 10　　(A)　　(B)　　(C)

Question 11　　(A)　　(B)　　(C)

Question 12　　(A)　　(B)　　(C)

Question 13　　(A)　　(B)　　(C)

Question 14　　(A)　　(B)　　(C)

Question 15　　(A)　　(B)　　(C)

Part B

Directions: You will now hear a series of short selections. You will hear them <u>only once</u> and they are not printed in your test booklet. After each selection, you will be asked one or more questions about what you have just heard. These questions, with four possible answers, are printed in your test booklet. Select the best answer to each question from among the four choices given and fill in the corresponding oval on your answer sheet. You will have 15 seconds to answer each question.

 # 16

<u>**Question 16**</u>   What kind of sports does Xiao Goa like?

(A)   He likes basketball only.

(B)   He likes all kinds of sports.

(C)   He hates all the sports.

(D)   He likes volleyball only.

 # 17

<u>**Question 17**</u>   Where does this conversation take place?

(A)   library

(B)   book Store

(C)   theater

(D)   restaurant

 # 18

<u>**Question 18**</u>   The person decided to sent the mail by

(A)   regular mail

(B)   express mail

(C)   registered mail

(D)   air mail

 # 19

<u>**Question 19**</u>   Who is coming this afternoon?

(A)   mother

(B)   brother

(C)   uncle

(D)   aunt

 # 20

<u>**Question 20**</u>   What day is today?

(A)   Wednesday

(B)   Thursday

(C)   Friday

(D)   Saturday

 # 21

Question 21   What did the customer not buy?

(A)   tea

(B)   cookies

(C)   soda

(D)   orange

 # 22

Question 22   What's the man's suggestion?

(A)   to borrow a dictionary from somewhere else

(B)   to buy a dictionary

(C)   to borrow a better dictionary

(D)   to take the dictionary home

 # 23

Question 23   What does the woman want?

(A)   to borrow a car

(B)   to go to the city with the man

(C)   to come home for dinner

(D)   let the man use her car

 # 24

Question 24   What is in the box?

(A)   It has nothing inside.

(B)   Nothing written on the cards.

(C)   There is nothing but cards.

(D)   He didn't take anything out from the box.

 # 25

Question 25   What does John mean?

(A)   Mary took the book.

(B)   Mary didn't take any book.

(C)   Mary took ten books.

(D)   Mary took nine books.

26
Question 26   Why didn't Lily go to class yesterday?

(A)   She was sick.

(B)   Her roommate was late.

(C)   Her roommate was lazy.

(D)   She had to take her roommate to the hospital.

27
Question 27   What is this conversation about?

(A)   asking for a bill in a restaurant

(B)   asking for a menu in a restaurant

(C)   asking a friend to pay for the bill

(D)   asking for the dessert menu in restaurant

28~30
Question 28   What does the man need?

(A)   to visit a friend in America

(B)   to ask for a phone number

(C)   to buy an airplane ticket

(D)   to make a long distance call

Question 29   According to the conversation, which country is the man not in?

(A)   Taiwan

(B)   China

(C)   Thailand

(D)   U.S.A.

Question 30   What will the man most likely do next?

(A)   get the phone number he need

(B)   get a plane ticket

(C)   give her the phone number

(D)   go to the airport

SAT II 中文模擬試題 第五套
Section I : Listening Comprehension

Part A

Directions: In this part of the test you will hear short questions, statements, or exchanges in Mandarin Chinese, followed by three responses designated (A), (B), and (C). You will hear the statements or questions, as well as the responses, just one time and they are not printed in your test booklet. Therefore, you must listen very carefully. Select the best response and fill in the corresponding oval on your answer sheet. You will have 15 seconds to answer each question.

Question 1

我們怎麼去中國城？

    (A) 中國城很遠。

    (B) 我們開車去吧！

    (C) 中國城裏有很多東西。

Question 2

他昨天爲什麼沒來學校？

    (A) 他爸爸送他來學校的。

    (B) 他是跟姐姐一起來的。

    (C) 因爲他生病了。

Question 3

我一來就麻煩您，眞不好意思。

    (A) 請慢用。

    (B) 哪裏！哪裏！

    (C) 恭喜您！

Question 4

你父親是做什麼的？

    (A) 他是坐飛機來的。

    (B) 他喜歡做菜。

    (C) 他是生意人。

Question 5

今年冬天比去年還冷，而且還冷得多。

    (A) 今年冬天有一點兒冷。

    (B) 今年冬天比較暖和。

    (C) 今年冬天特別冷。

Question 6

他說走就走，連句再見都沒說。

    (A) 他眞是太沒禮貌了。

    (B) 他眞是不錯。

    (C) 他眞是太有意思了。

Question 7

小楊一坐就是兩個小時，吃得好痛快。

    (A)小楊吃得很高興。

    (B)小楊吃得很快。

    (C)小楊吃得胃痛。

Question 8

排隊買票划船的人太多，我們今天還是別去了。

    (A)他們不會划船。

    (B)他們怕買不到票。

    (C)他們太懶了。

Question 9

我吃完飯了，得先上樓去做功課了。

    (A)請大家隨便坐。

    (B)請大家快吃。

    (C)請大家慢用。

Question 10

李安的電影〝臥虎藏龍〞，我看了六遍，你呢？

    (A)我看了〝推手〞。

    (B)李安是華裔導演。

    (C)八遍。

Question 11

聽說北大暑期中文班越辦越好，還會去黃山旅遊，你報名了嗎？

    (A)我有朋友在北大學中文。

    (B)黃山美極了。

    (C)我已經報名了。

Question 12

你昨天去看熊貓<u>美香</u>和<u>天天</u>了，對嗎？

    (A) 熊貓真討人喜歡。

    (B) 沒錯，我和家人一起去的。

    (C) 他下星期日去。

Question 13

烈日當空，你還穿這麼厚的工作服，難怪全身汗水流個不停。這句話適用於哪個季節？

    (A) 冬季

    (B) 夏季

    (C) 春季

Question 14

在美國吃日本菜比較貴，中國菜的價錢就比較公道。

    (A) 中國菜比較便宜。

    (B) 中國菜比較受歡迎。

    (C) 中國菜比較好吃。

Question 15

想要把李小明的微波爐修好，那還不容易。

    (A) 太不容易了。

    (B) 不太容易。

    (C) 太容易了。

Part B

Directions: You will now hear a series of short selections. You will hear them <u>only once</u> and they are not printed in your test booklet. After each selection, you will be asked one or more questions about what you have just heard. These questions, with four possible answers, are printed in your test booklet. Select the best answer to each question from among the four choices given and fill in the corresponding oval on your answer sheet. You will have 15 seconds to answer each question.

Question 16

女：小高，你喜歡打排球嗎？

男：所有的運動，沒有我不喜歡的。

Question 17

女：我想找一本有關美國南北戰爭的書。

男：我們有很多，你要指定特別的作者嗎？

女：不需要。

男：你看這一本，好不好？

女：我先買了再說，你們這裏可以退書嗎？

Question 18

女：先生，從舊金山寄一封信到紐約要幾天？

男：平信三天，快信只要一天。

女：我希望越快越好，那就寄快信吧，要貼多少錢的郵票？

男：兩塊錢。

Question 19

女：阿姨今天下午從上海來美國，我要到機場去接她。

男：她的飛機幾點到？

女：下午三點半。

男：哪一個機場？

女：舊金山國際機場。

Question 20

女：這個星期六，學校有一場精彩的足球賽。

男：什麼時候開始賣票。

女：開賽的前一天開始賣票。

男：明天我有課，你能幫我買票嗎？

Question 21

女：老闆，來三瓶汽水，兩磅橘子，五包餅乾，一共多少錢？

男：一共九塊半，還要些什麼嗎？

女：不要了，謝謝。

Question 22

女：我的法文老師要我來借一本字典。

男：可以，但是不能帶出去。

女：那不是很不方便嗎？

男：是啊，我建議你自己去買一本。

Question 23

女：你今天用不用車？我想進城買東西。

男：你要用就開去吧，只要在晚飯以前回來就行。

Question 24

男：打開盒子，看看裏面放了些什麼東西？

女：除了卡片以外，什麼都沒有。

Question 25

女：約翰，你看到我放在桌上的那本小說嗎？

男：沒有，不過我想十之八九是被瑪麗拿去了。

Question 26

男：莉莉，昨天你爲什麼沒去上課？

女：我的室友感冒了，我送她去醫院。

Question 27

男：小姐，請把帳單給我。

女：吃飽了嗎？要不要來點甜點？

男：不要了，謝謝！

女：好，請等一下！

女：這是你的帳單，下次請再來。

Question 28~30

男：接線生，請幫我接一通國際長途電話。

女：好的，請問您要打到哪個國家？

男：美國。

女：請把您要打的電話號碼告訴我。

Section II : Grammar

Directions: This section consists of a number of incomplete statements, each of which has four suggested completions. Select the word or phrase that best completes the sentence structurally and logically. Please fill in the corresponding oval on the answer sheet.

THE QUESTIONS ARE PRESENTED IN FOUR DIFFERENT WRITING SYSTEMS: TRADITIONAL CHARACTERS, SIMPLIFIED CHARACTERS, PINYIN ROMANIZATION, AND CHINESE PHONETIC ALPHABET(BO PO MO FO). TO SAVE TIME, IT IS RECOMMENDED THAT YOU CHOOSE THE WRITING SYSTEM WITH WHICH YOU ARE MOST FAMILIAR WITH AND **READ ONLY THAT VERSION OF THE QUESTION.**

31. 請你＿＿＿寫封信給他。

    (A) 抽風

    (B) 抽中

    (C) 抽樣

    (D) 抽空

31. 请你＿＿＿写封信给他。

    (A) 抽风

    (B) 抽中

    (C) 抽样

    (D) 抽空

31. ㄑㄧㄥ ㄋㄧ ＿＿＿ ㄒㄧㄝ ㄈㄥ ㄒㄧㄣ ㄍㄟ ㄊㄚ。

    (A) ㄔㄡ ㄈㄥ

    (B) ㄔㄡ ㄓㄨㄥ

    (C) ㄔㄡ ㄧㄤ

    (D) ㄔㄡ ㄎㄨㄥ

31. Qǐng nǐ ＿＿＿ xiě fēng xìn gěi tā.

    (A) chōu fēng

    (B) chōu zhòng

    (C) chōu yàng

    (D) chōu kòng

---

32. 這條高速公路，＿＿＿上下班時間一定塞車。

    (A) 每到

    (B) 可是

    (C) 每時

    (D) 沒有

32. 这条高速公路，＿＿＿上下班时间一定塞车。

    (A) 每到

    (B) 可是

    (C) 每时

    (D) 没有

32. ㄓㄜ ㄊㄧㄠ ㄍㄠ ㄙㄨ ㄍㄨㄥ ㄌㄨ，＿＿＿ ㄕㄤ ㄒㄧㄚ ㄅㄢ ㄕ ㄐㄧㄢ ㄧ ㄉㄧㄥ ㄙㄞ ㄔㄜ。

    (A) ㄇㄟ ㄉㄠ

    (B) ㄎㄜ ㄕ

    (C) ㄇㄟ ㄕ

    (D) ㄇㄟ ㄧㄡ

32. Zhè tiáo gāo sù gōng lù, ＿＿＿ shàng xià bān shí jiān yí dìng sāi chē.

    (A) měi dào

    (B) kě shì

    (C) měi shí

    (D) méi yǒu

33. 沒想到他___回絕了我的好意。

    (A) 一心

    (B) 一同

    (C) 一起

    (D) 一口

33. 没想到他___回绝了我的好意。

    (A) 一心

    (B) 一同

    (C) 一起

    (D) 一口

33. Méi xiǎng dào tā ___ huí jué le wǒ de hǎo yì.

    (A) yì xīn

    (B) yì tóng

    (C) yì qǐ

    (D) yì kǒu

---

34. 弟弟投籃，___投得太低，___投得太高。

    (A) 不是…就是

    (B) 是…可是

    (C) 只是…總是

    (D) 是…還是

34. 弟弟投篮，___投得太低，___投得太高。

    (A) 不是---就是

    (B) 是---可是

    (C) 只是---总是

    (D) 是---还是

34. Dì di tóu lán, ___ tóu de tài dī, ___ tóu de tài gāo.

    (A) bú shì…jiù shì

    (B) shì…kě shì

    (C) zhǐ shì…zǒng shì

    (D) shì…hái shì

---

35. 爸爸今天___早飯___沒吃，就去公司開會了。

    (A) 一…就

    (B) 連…都

    (C) 雖然…但是

    (D) 不跟…一樣

35. 爸爸今天___早饭___没吃，就去公司开会了。

    (A) 一---就

    (B) 连---都

    (C) 虽然---但是

    (D) 不跟----一样

35. Bà ba jīn tiān ___ zǎo fàn ___ méi chī, jiù qù gōng sī kāi huì le.

    (A) yì…jiù

    (B) lián…dōu

    (C) suī rán…dàn shì

    (D) bù gēn…yí yàng

36. 星期六家裏請客，來的人＿＿＿，很熱鬧。

    (A) 不多

    (B) 很少

    (C) 太少

    (D) 不少

36. 星期六家裏请客，来的人＿＿＿，很热闹。

    (A) 不多

    (B) 很少

    (C) 太少

    (D) 不少

36. Xīng qí liù jiā lǐ qǐng kè, lái de rén ___, hěn rè nào.

    (A) bù duō

    (B) hěn shǎo

    (C) tài shǎo

    (D) bù shǎo

---

37. 哪怕困難再多，我＿＿＿放棄這個計劃。

    (A) 決心

    (B) 決定

    (C) 決不

    (D) 決議

37. 哪怕困难再多，我＿＿＿放弃这个计划。

    (A) 决心

    (B) 决定

    (C) 决不

    (D) 决议

37. Nǎ pà kùn nán zài duō, wǒ ___ fàng qì zhè ge jì huà.

    (A) jué xīn

    (B) jué dìng

    (C) jué bù

    (D) jué yì

---

38. 讓我們也聽聽別人的看法，＿＿＿＿＿＿ 他說的就是對的。

    (A) 不得了

    (B) 不由得

    (C) 不見得

    (D) 不得不

38. 让我们也听听别人的看法，＿＿＿＿＿＿ 他说的就是对的。

    (A) 不得了

    (B) 不由得

    (C) 不见得

    (D) 不得不

38. Ràng wǒ men yě tīng tīng bié rén de kàn fǎ, ＿＿＿＿ tā shuō de jiù shì duì de.

    (A) bù dé liǎo

    (B) bù yóu dé

    (C) bú jiàn dé

    (D) bù dé bù

39. 這條路彎彎曲曲的，開車＿＿＿要小心。

    (A) 萬一
    (B) 千萬
    (C) 一萬
    (D) 萬千

39. 这条路弯弯曲曲的，开车＿＿＿要小心。

    (A) 万一
    (B) 千万
    (C) 一万
    (D) 万千

39. Zhè tiáo lù wān wān qū qū de, kāi chē ＿＿＿ yào xiǎo xīn.

    (A) wàn yī
    (B) qiān wàn
    (C) yí wàn
    (D) wàn qiān

40. 她那粗心大意的個性，實在叫人＿＿＿＿＿。

    (A) 受得了
    (B) 受不了
    (C) 不得了
    (D) 免不了

40. 她那粗心大意的个性，实在叫人＿＿＿

    (A) 受得了
    (B) 受不了
    (C) 不得了
    (D) 免不了

40. Tā nà cū xīn dà yì de gè xìng, shí zài jiào rén ＿＿＿＿.

    (A) shòu dé liǎo
    (B) shòu bù liǎo
    (C) bù dé liǎo
    (D) miǎn bù liǎo

41. 你猜這＿＿＿飯，我們吃了多久？

    (A) 場
    (B) 片
    (C) 頓
    (D) 道

41. 你猜这＿＿＿饭，我们吃了多久？

    (A) 场
    (B) 片
    (C) 顿
    (D) 道

41. Nǐ cāi zhè ＿＿＿ fàn, wǒ men chī le duó jiǔ?

    (A) chǎng
    (B) piàn
    (C) dùn
    (D) dào

42. _____ 王大中竟然先走了！

    (A) 可能是

    (B) 不一定

    (C) 沒想到

    (D) 應該是

42. _____ ㄨㄤˊ ㄉㄚˋ ㄓㄨㄥ ㄐㄧㄥˋ ㄖㄢˊ ㄒㄧㄢ ㄗㄡˇ ㄌㄜ ！

    (A) ㄎㄜˇ ㄋㄥˊ ㄕˋ

    (B) ㄅㄨˋ ㄧˊ ㄉㄧㄥˋ

    (C) ㄇㄟˊ ㄒㄧㄤˇ ㄉㄠˋ

    (D) ㄧㄥ ㄍㄞ ㄕˋ

42. _____ 王大中竟然先走了！

    (A) 可能是

    (B) 不一定

    (C) 没想到

    (D) 应该是

42. _____ Wángdàzhōng jìng rán xiān zǒu le!

    (A) Kě néng shì

    (B) Bù yí dìng

    (C) Méi xiǎng dào

    (D) Yīng gāi shì

---

43. 妹妹 ____ 走著，____ 唱著歌。

    (A) 一樣是…還有一樣是

    (B) 應該…也應該

    (C) 十分…十分

    (D) 一邊…一邊

43. ㄇㄟˋ ㄇㄟ ____ ㄗㄡˇ ㄓㄜ ，____ ㄔㄤˋ ㄓㄜ ㄍㄜ 。

    (A) ㄧˊ ㄧㄤˋ ㄕˋ … ㄏㄞˊ ㄧㄡˇ ㄧˊ ㄧㄤˋ ㄕˋ

    (B) ㄧㄥ ㄍㄞ … ㄧㄝˇ ㄧㄥ ㄍㄞ

    (C) ㄕˊ ㄈㄣ … ㄕˊ ㄈㄣ

    (D) ㄧˊ ㄅㄧㄢ … ㄧˊ ㄅㄧㄢ

43. 妹妹 ____ 走著，____ 唱著歌。

    (A) 一样是…还有一样是

    (B) 应该…也应该

    (C) 十分…十分

    (D) 一边…一边

43. Mèi mei ____ zǒu zhe, ____ chàng zhe gē.

    (A) yí yàng shì .... hái yǒu yí yàng shì

    (B) yīng gāi .... yě yīng gāi

    (C) shí fēn .... shí fēn

    (D) yì biān .... yì biān

---

44. 如果我也能參加籃球校隊，那 __ 有多好呀！

    (A) 還

    (B) 才

    (C) 也

    (D) 該

44. ㄖㄨˊ ㄍㄨㄛˇ ㄨㄛˇ ㄧㄝˇ ㄋㄥˊ ㄘㄢ ㄐㄧㄚ ㄌㄢˊ ㄑㄧㄡˊ ㄒㄧㄠˋ ㄉㄨㄟˋ ， ㄋㄚˋ __ ㄧㄡˇ ㄉㄨㄛ ㄏㄠˇ ㄧㄚ ！

    (A) ㄏㄞˊ

    (B) ㄘㄞˊ

    (C) ㄧㄝˇ

    (D) ㄍㄞ

44. 如果我也能参加籃球校队，那 __ 有多好呀！

    (A) 还

    (B) 才

    (C) 也

    (D) 该

44. Rú guǒ wǒ yě néng cān jiā lán qiú xiào duì, nà ____ yǒu duó hǎo ya!

    (A) hái

    (B) cái

    (C) yě

    (D) gāi

45. 王小明一個人先走了，___丁大中也
    走了。
    (A) 還是
    (B) 以外
    (C) 只是
    (D) 接著

45. 王小明一個人先走了，___丁大中也
    走了。
    (A) 还是
    (B) 以外
    (C) 只是
    (D) 接著

45. ㄨㄤˊ ㄒㄧㄠˇ ㄇㄧㄥˊ ㄧˊ ㄍㄜ ㄖㄣˊ ㄒㄧㄢ ㄗㄡˇ ㄌㄜ， ___ ㄉㄧㄥ ㄉㄚˋ ㄓㄨㄥ ㄧㄝˇ ㄗㄡˇ ㄌㄜ。
    (A) ㄏㄞˊ ㄕˋ
    (B) ㄧˇ ㄨㄞˋ
    (C) ㄓˇ ㄕˋ
    (D) ㄐㄧㄝ ㄓㄜ

45. Wángxiǎomíng yí ge rén xiān zǒu le, _____ Dīngdàzhōng yě zǒu le.
    (A) hái shì
    (B) yǐ wài
    (C) zhǐ shì
    (D) jiē zhe

46. 這件事___王大中去做，____李小明
    去做，不用擔心。
    (A) 是…就是
    (B) 不是…還是
    (C) 不是…就是
    (D) 不是…也是

46. 这件事___王大中去做，____李小明
    去做，不用担心。
    (A) 是---就是
    (B) 不是---还是
    (C) 不是---就是
    (D) 不是---也是

46. ㄓㄜˋ ㄐㄧㄢˋ ㄕˋ ___ ㄨㄤˊ ㄉㄚˋ ㄓㄨㄥ ㄑㄩˋ ㄗㄨㄛˋ， ___ ㄌㄧˇ ㄒㄧㄠˇ ㄇㄧㄥˊ ㄑㄩˋ ㄗㄨㄛˋ，ㄅㄨˊ ㄩㄥˋ ㄉㄢ ㄒㄧㄣ。
    (A) ㄕˋ …ㄐㄧㄡˋ ㄕˋ
    (B) ㄅㄨˊ ㄕˋ …ㄏㄞˊ ㄕˋ
    (C) ㄅㄨˊ ㄕˋ …ㄐㄧㄡˋ ㄕˋ
    (D) ㄅㄨˊ ㄕˋ …ㄧㄝˇ ㄕˋ

46. Zhè jiàn shì ___ Wángdàzhōng qù zuò, ____ Lǐxiǎomíng qù zuò, bú yòng dān xīn.
    (A) shì...jiù shì
    (B) bú shì...hái shì
    (C) bú shì...jiù shì
    (D) bú shì...yě shì

47. 你看過這本漫畫書嗎？____有趣的。
    (A) 才
    (B) 必
    (C) 恰
    (D) 怪

47. 你看过这本漫画书吗？____有趣的。
    (A) 才
    (B) 必
    (C) 恰
    (D) 怪

47. ㄋㄧˇ ㄎㄢˋ ㄍㄨㄛˋ ㄓㄜˋ ㄅㄣˇ ㄇㄢˋ ㄏㄨㄚˋ ㄕㄨ ㄇㄚ？ ___ ㄧㄡˇ ㄑㄩˋ ㄉㄜ。
    (A) ㄘㄞˊ
    (B) ㄅㄧˋ
    (C) ㄑㄧㄚˋ
    (D) ㄍㄨㄞˋ

47. Nǐ kàn guò zhè běn màn huà shū ma? ___ yǒu qù de.
    (A) cái
    (B) bì
    (C) qià
    (D) guài

139

48. 這次的考試實在＿＿難了，我考得很差。

    (A) 不
    (B) 也
    (C) 就
    (D) 太

48. 这次的考试实在＿＿难了，我考得很差。

    (A) 不
    (B) 也
    (C) 就
    (D) 太

48. ㄓㄜˋ ㄘˋ ㄉㄜ˙ ㄎㄠˇ ㄕˋ ㄕˊ ㄗㄞˋ ＿＿ ㄋㄢˊ ㄌㄜ˙，ㄨㄛˇ ㄎㄠˇ ㄉㄜ˙ ㄏㄣˇ ㄔㄚˋ。

    (A) ㄅㄨˋ
    (B) ㄧㄝˇ
    (C) ㄐㄧㄡˋ
    (D) ㄊㄞˋ

48. Zhè cì de kǎo shì shí zài ＿＿ nán le, wǒ kǎo de hěn chà.

    (A) bù
    (B) yě
    (C) jiù
    (D) tài

---

49. 這幾天的天氣＿＿，如果不小心穿衣服，很容易生病。

    (A) 暖洋洋的
    (B) 熱烘烘的
    (C) 忽冷忽熱的
    (D) 剛剛好

49. 这几天的天气＿＿，如果不小心穿衣服，很容易生病。

    (A) 暖洋洋的
    (B) 热烘烘的
    (C) 忽冷忽热的
    (D) 刚刚好

49. ㄓㄜˋ ㄐㄧˇ ㄊㄧㄢ ㄉㄜ˙ ㄊㄧㄢ ㄑㄧˋ ＿＿，ㄖㄨˊ ㄍㄨㄛˇ ㄅㄨˋ ㄒㄧㄠˇ ㄒㄧㄣ ㄔㄨㄢ ㄧ ㄈㄨˊ，ㄏㄣˇ ㄖㄨㄥˊ ㄧˋ ㄕㄥ ㄅㄧㄥˋ。

    (A) ㄋㄨㄢˇ ㄧㄤˊ ㄧㄤˊ ㄉㄜ˙
    (B) ㄖㄜˋ ㄏㄨㄥ ㄏㄨㄥ ㄉㄜ˙
    (C) ㄏㄨ ㄌㄥˇ ㄏㄨ ㄖㄜˋ ㄉㄜ˙
    (D) ㄍㄤ ㄍㄤ ㄏㄠˇ

49. Zhè jǐ tiān de tiān qì ＿＿, rú guǒ bù xiǎo xīn chuān yī fú, hěn róng yì shēng bìng.

    (A) nuǎn yáng yáng de
    (B) rè hōng hōng de
    (C) hū lěng hū rè de
    (D) gāng gāng hǎo

---

50. ＿＿太緊張，＿＿她考試失常了。

    (A) 實在…以為
    (B) 由於…所以
    (C) 因為…只是
    (D) 就是…可以

50. ＿＿太紧张，＿＿她考试失常了。

    (A) 实在…以为
    (B) 由於…所以
    (C) 因为…只是
    (D) 就是…可以

50. ＿＿ ㄊㄞˋ ㄐㄧㄣˇ ㄓㄤ，＿＿ ㄊㄚ ㄎㄠˇ ㄕˋ ㄕ ㄔㄤˊ ㄌㄜ˙。

    (A) ㄕˊ ㄗㄞˋ … ㄧˇ ㄨㄟˊ
    (B) ㄧㄡˊ ㄩˊ … ㄙㄨㄛˇ ㄧˇ
    (C) ㄧㄣ ㄨㄟˋ … ㄓˇ ㄕˋ
    (D) ㄐㄧㄡˋ ㄕˋ … ㄎㄜˇ ㄧˇ

50. ＿＿ tài jǐn zhāng, ＿＿ tā kǎo shì shī cháng le.

    (A) shí zài … yǐ wéi
    (B) yóu yú … suǒ yǐ
    (C) yīn wèi … zhǐ shì
    (D) jiù shì … kě yǐ

51. 博愛中文學校的學生每個星期六上午要上幾____中文課？

(A) 朵
(B) 頓
(C) 排
(D) 堂

51. 博爱中文学校的学生每个星期六上午要上几____中文课？

(A) 朵
(B) 顿
(C) 排
(D) 堂

51. ㄅㄛˊ ㄞˋ ㄓㄨㄥ ㄨㄣˊ ㄒㄩㄝˊ ㄒㄧㄠˋ ㄉㄜ˙ ㄒㄩㄝˊ ㄕㄥ ㄇㄟˇ ㄍㄜ˙ ㄒㄧㄥ ㄑㄧˊ ㄌㄧㄡˋ ㄕㄤˋ ㄨˇ ㄧㄠˋ ㄕㄤˋ ㄐㄧˇ ____ ㄓㄨㄥ ㄨㄣˊ ㄎㄜˋ ？

(A) ㄉㄨㄛˇ
(B) ㄉㄨㄣˋ
(C) ㄆㄞˊ
(D) ㄊㄤˊ

51. Bóài Zhōngwén xué xiào de xué shēng měi ge xīng qí liù shàng wǔ yào shàng jǐ ____ Zhōngwén kè ?

(A) duǒ
(B) dùn
(C) pái
(D) táng

---

52. 最近天氣不好，____天天都下雨。

(A) 從來
(B) 從不
(C) 幾許
(D) 幾乎

52. 最近天气不好，____天天都下雨。

(A) 从来
(B) 从不
(C) 几许
(D) 几乎

52. ㄗㄨㄟˋ ㄐㄧㄣˋ ㄊㄧㄢ ㄑㄧˋ ㄅㄨˋ ㄏㄠˇ ，____ ㄊㄧㄢ ㄊㄧㄢ ㄉㄡ ㄒㄧㄚˋ ㄩˇ 。

(A) ㄘㄨㄥˊ ㄌㄞˊ
(B) ㄘㄨㄥˊ ㄅㄨˋ
(C) ㄐㄧˇ ㄒㄩˇ
(D) ㄐㄧ ㄏㄨ

52. Zuì jìn tiān qì bù hǎo, ____ tiān tiān dōu xià yǔ.

(A) cóng lái
(B) cóng bù
(C) jǐ xǔ
(D) jī hū

---

53. 這麼好的文章，____讚美嗎？

(A) 可以
(B) 可能
(C) 能不
(D) 可不

53. 这麼好的文章，____讚美吗？

(A) 可以
(B) 可能
(C) 能不
(D) 可不

53. ㄓㄜˋ ㄇㄜ˙ ㄏㄠˇ ㄉㄜ˙ ㄨㄣˊ ㄓㄤ ，____ ㄗㄢˋ ㄇㄟˇ ㄇㄚ˙ ？

(A) ㄎㄜˇ ㄧˇ
(B) ㄎㄜˇ ㄋㄥˊ
(C) ㄋㄥˊ ㄅㄨˊ
(D) ㄎㄜˇ ㄅㄨˊ

53. Zhè me hǎo de wén zhāng, ____ zàng měi ma ?

(A) kě yǐ
(B) kě néng
(C) néng bú
(D) kě bú

54. 你如果＿＿＿不安靜聽課，老師就要叫
你到外面罰站了。

　　(A) 重
　　(B) 會
　　(C) 再
　　(D) 也

54. 你如果＿＿＿不安静听课，老师就要叫
你到外面罚站了。

　　(A) 重
　　(B) 会
　　(C) 再
　　(D) 也

54. ㄋㄧˇ ㄖㄨˊ ＿＿＿ ㄅㄨˋ ㄢ ㄐㄧㄥˋ ㄊㄧㄥ ㄎㄜˋ，ㄌㄠˇ ㄕ ㄐㄧㄡˋ ㄧㄠˋ ㄐㄧㄠˋ ㄋㄧˇ ㄉㄠˋ ㄨㄞˋ ㄇㄧㄢˋ ㄈㄚˊ ㄓㄢˋ ㄌㄜ。

　　(A) ㄓㄨㄥˋ
　　(B) ㄏㄨㄟˋ
　　(C) ㄗㄞˋ
　　(D) ㄧㄝˇ

54. Nǐ rú guǒ ＿＿＿ bù ān jìng tīng kè, lǎo shī jiù yào jiào nǐ dào wài miàn fá zhàn le.

　　(A) zhòng
　　(B) huì
　　(C) zài
　　(D) yě

---

55. 弟弟＿＿＿念了幾分鐘的書，＿＿＿吵著
要出去玩了。

　　(A) 有…也
　　(B) 只…沒
　　(C) 才…就
　　(D) 是…可

55. 弟弟＿＿＿念了几分钟的书，＿＿＿吵著
要出去玩了。

　　(A) 有---也
　　(B) 只---没
　　(C) 才---就
　　(D) 是---可

55. ㄉㄧˋ ㄉㄧ ＿＿＿ ㄋㄧㄢˋ ㄌㄜ ㄐㄧˇ ㄈㄣ ㄓㄨㄥ ㄉㄜ ㄕㄨ，＿＿＿ ㄔㄠˇ ㄓㄜ ㄧㄠˋ ㄔㄨ ㄑㄩˋ ㄨㄢˊ ㄌㄜ。

　　(A) ㄧㄡˇ …ㄧㄝˇ
　　(B) ㄓˇ …ㄇㄟˊ
　　(C) ㄘㄞˊ …ㄐㄧㄡˋ
　　(D) ㄕˋ …ㄎㄜˇ

55. Dì di ＿＿＿ niàn le jǐ fēn zhōng de shū, ＿＿＿ chǎo zhe yào chū qù wán le.

　　(A) yǒu ...yě
　　(B) zhǐ ...méi
　　(C) cái ... jiù
　　(D) shì ... kě

SAT II 中文模擬試題 第五套
Section III : Reading Comprehension

Directions: Read the following selections carefully for comprehension. Each selection is followed by one or more questions or incomplete statements based on its content. Select the answer or completion that is best according to the passage and fill in the corresponding oval on the answer sheet.
THIS SECTION OF THE TEST IS PRESENTED IN TWO WRITING SYSTEMS: TRADITIONAL CHARACTERS AND SIMPLIFIED CHARACTERS. IT IS RECOMMENDED THAT YOU CHOOSE ONLY THAT WRITING SYSTEM WITH WHICH YOU ARE MOST FAMILIAR AS YOU WORK THROUGH THIS SECTION OF THE TEST.

56~58

五月五，端午節，吃粽子，賽龍舟。敲鑼打鼓好熱鬧！	五月五，端午节，吃粽子，赛龙舟。敲锣打鼓好热闹！

Question 56   Whom are we remembering on this festival?
(A) The greatest teacher, Confucius
(B) Mencius
(C) A noble Chinese poet, Qu Yuan
(D) The great poet, Li Bai

Question 57   What are we eating on this holiday?
(A) fish balls
(B) rice cake
(C) rice tamale
(D) moon cake

Question 58   What date is the Dragon Boat Festival?
(A) May 15, Western calendar
(B) May 5, Chinese calendar
(C) May 5, Western calendar
(D) August 15, Chinese calendar

59~60

请来品嚐我們特地爲您準備
的柳丁、橘子、葡萄柚及多種不
同的柑橘品種。

如果您有任何栽培上的困難
，我們有説中文的園藝專家，在
此替您解答。

请来品尝我们特地为您准备
的柳丁、桔子、葡萄柚及多种不
同的柑桔品种。

如果您有任何栽培上的困难
，我们有说中文的园艺专家，在
此替您解答。

Question 59   This advertisement was likely placed by a(n) _____ .

     (A)   farm

     (B)   winery

     (C)   tree pruning company

     (D)   orchard

Question 60   The company is specialized in growing _____ .

     (A)   oranges

     (B)   apples

     (C)   grapes

     (D)   cherries

61

購物中心

共15家商店。包括：Safeway超級市場、
辦公室用品店、美容用品店、服裝店、
花店、玩具店、電器用品店等等。

购物中心

共15家商店。包括：Safeway超级市场、
办公室用品店、美容用品店、服装店、
花店、玩具店、电器用品店等等。

Question 61   What shop or store can not be found in this square?

     (A)   toy store

     (B)   book store

     (C)   flower shop

     (D)   office supply shop

62

旺來小吃

可口合菜・經濟實惠・堂食外賣
一律歡迎

晚餐贈券

憑券優待，每日十客，先到先得
優待至2001年2月16日止

旺来小吃

可口合菜・经济实惠・堂食外卖
一律欢迎

晚餐赠券

凭券优待，每日十客，先到先得
优待至2001年2月16日止

Question 62　　What is this?

    (A)　a coupon

    (B)　a receipt

    (C)　an order form

    (D)　a service rating form

63~64

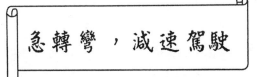

急轉彎，減速駕駛

急转弯，减速驾驶

Question 63　　The sign is most relevant to whom?

    (A)　pedestrians

    (B)　consumers

    (C)　drivers

    (D)　none of the above

Question 64　　The purpose of this sign is for:

    (A)　directions

    (B)　parking restrictions

    (C)　advertisement

    (D)　a warning sign for road conditions

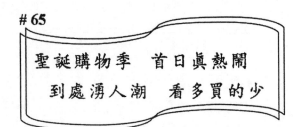

65

聖誕購物季　首日真熱鬧
到處湧人潮　看多買的少

圣诞购物季　首日真热闹
到处湧人潮　看多买的少

Question 65　　　The headline is about_____

    (A)　　a Christmas gift

    (B)　　an after Christmas sale

    (C)　　a Christmas greeting

    (D)　　a Christmas shopping season

66~68

臺北火車站各部門的電話：	
服務台	: 2735 -1491
人事處	: 2735 -1492
醫務室	: 2735 -1493
失物招領	: 2735 -1494
訂購月票	: 2735 -1495
查詢班車時刻	: 2735 -1496

台北火车站各部门的电话：	
服务臺	: 2735 -1491
人事处	: 2735 -1492
医务室	: 2735 -1493
失物招领	: 2735 -1494
订购月票	: 2735 -1495
查询班车时刻	: 2735 -1496

Question 66　　　What is the phone number for Lost and Found?

    (A)　　2735 -1491

    (B)　　2735 -1496

    (C)　　2735 -1494

    (D)　　2735 -1495

Question 67　　　To purchase a monthly pass, you should call_____

    (A)　　2735 -1495

    (B)　　2735 -1492

    (C)　　2735 -1493

    (D)　　2735 -1491

Question 68   What number do you call for train schedules?

(A)   2735 -1494

(B)   2735 -1492

(C)   2735 -1493

(D)   2735 -1496

69~70

舊金山現代藝術博物館	旧金山现代艺术博物馆
本館以現代畫、雕刻和現代攝影名聞遐邇。館內設有書店	本馆以现代画、雕刻和现代摄影名闻遐迩。馆内设有书店
※開放時間	※开放时间
週二、三、五　10:00 am - 5:00 pm	週二、三、五　10:00 am - 5:00 pm
週四　　　　　10:00 am - 9:00 pm	週四　　　　　10:00 am - 9:00 pm
週六、日　　　11:00 am - 5:00 pm	週六、日　　　11:00 am - 5:00 pm
★半價優惠—每月第一個	★半价优惠—每月第一个
星期二 (10:00 am - 5:00 pm) 星期四 (10:00 am - 5:00 pm)	星期二 (10:00 am - 5:00 pm) 星期四 (10:00 am - 5:00 pm)

Question 69   This is a museum of _____

(A)   contemporary art

(B)   Eastern art

(C)   ancient art

(D)   Asian art

Question 70   If you go to the museum on the first Tuesday of the month, _____

(A)   the admission is free

(B)   the admission is half price

(C)   there is a tour guide

(D)   it is closed

包餃子晚會

歡迎今年新來的同學！下星期六晚上五時，在大學餐廳舉行一年一次的新生包餃子晚會。晚會上餐廳將供應包餃子的材料及各種飲料。各人包自己的餃子，多吃多包，少吃少包，餐廳廚房的服務人員負責煮餃子。歡迎所有的同學和老師都來參加。門票每人五元，在大學書店預售。

包饺子晚会

欢迎今年新来的同学！下星期六晚上五时，在大学餐厅举行一年一次的新生包饺子晚会。晚会上餐厅将供应包饺子的材料及各种饮料。各人包自己的饺子，多吃多包，少吃少包，餐厅厨房的服务人员负责煮饺子。欢迎所有的同学和老师都来参加。门票每人五元，在大学书店预售。

Question 71   The flyer announces that there will be a _____.

(A)   potluck party

(B)   dinner party

(C)   dumpling making party

(D)   farewell party

Question 72   The party welcomes _____ to attend.

(A)   only new students

(B)   returning as well as new students

(C)   new students and new teachers

(D)   all students and teachers

Question 73   To attend the party you need to _____.

(A)   bring dumpling wrappers

(B)   bring dumpling ingredients

(C)   purchase a ticket

(D)   bring your own dumplings

Question 74   How often the party is held?

    (A)   every semester

    (B)   once a year

    (C)   every Saturday during the school year

    (D)   irregularly

75~77

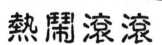

熱鬧滾滾

四校聯合舞會

Fri. Feb. 23, 8:00 pm - 1:00 am

@世界日報活動中心

热闹滚滚

四校联合舞会

Fri. Feb. 23, 8:00 pm - 1:00 am

@世界日报活动中心

Question 75   What does the event of this announcement refer to?

    (A)   a birthday party

    (B)   a school orientation

    (C)   a dance party

    (D)   a high school reunion

Question 76   How many schools sponsor this event?

    (A)   one

    (B)   two

    (C)   three

    (D)   four

這個公園的特色是海邊的沙丘和野花、可騎單車的小徑、海灣的活動中心，而且還提供了各式各樣的展覽及有教育性的海洋資訊。可供活動項目有野餐、烤肉、打球、游泳、滑水、釣魚、看鳥，每年六月受歡迎的堆沙堡比賽也在此舉行。

这个公园的特色是海边的沙丘和野花、可骑单车的小径、海湾的活动中心，而且还提供了各式各样的展览及有教育性的海洋资讯。可供活动项目有野餐、烤肉、打球、游泳、滑水、钓鱼、看鸟，每年六月受欢迎的堆沙堡比赛也在此举行。

Question 77　　Which of the following recreational activities is not mentioned in the passage?

(A)　swimming

(B)　fishing

(C)　boating

(D)　bird watch

Question 78　　The park is right by _____.

(A)　a river

(B)　the ocean

(C)　a lake

(D)　a reservoir

Question 79　　Every June there is a _____ contest held here.

(A)　fishing

(B)　swimming

(C)　water-skiing

(D)　sand castle building

80

郵購訂購單	
姓名	
地址	
電話	( )＿＿＿
付款方式	○現金　○支票
品名	

邮购订购单	
姓名	
地址	
电话	( )＿＿＿
付款方式	○现金　○支票
品名	

Question 80

What is this?

(A)　a registered mail receipt

(B)　a mail order form

(C)　a mailing label

(D)　a subscription form

百貨公司年終大減價
童裝七折 女裝六折 男裝八折
其他物品一律七五折

百貨公司年終大減价
童裝七折 女裝六折 男裝八折
其他物品一律七五折

Question 81

Mary wants to buy a dress, what discount will she receive?

(A)　60% off

(B)　30% off

(C)　40% off

(D)　20% off

Question 82

Dad is going to buy a new suit, it was $250.00, what is the sale price?

(A)　$175.00

(B)　$200.00

(C)　$150.00

(D)　none of the above

Question 83

Mom bought a toaster, what discount did she receive?

(A) 70% off

(B) 30% off

(C) 75% off

(D) 25% off

84~85

華人社區溝通　普通話成主流

紐約、金山、洛城華埠
廣東話逐漸褪流行

在華埠　國語　普通話當道
會說普通話　國語
走遍華埠都不怕

華人社區沟通　普通话成主流

纽约、金山、洛城华埠
广东话逐渐褪流行

在华埠　国语　普通话当道
会说普通话　国语
走遍华埠都不怕

Question 84

According to the article, what is the most popular dialect currently used in American Chinatowns ?

(A) Shanghainese

(B) Cantonese

(C) Mandarin

(D) Taiwanese

Question 85

In the past, the most commonly spoken dialect in most Chinatowns was_____.

(A) Taiwanese

(B) Cantonese

(C) Shanghainese

(D) Mandarin

SAT II 中文模擬試卷 第六套
Section I : Listening Comprehension

Part A

Directions: In this part of the test you will hear short questions, statements, or exchanges in Mandarin Chinese, follow by three responses designated (A), (B), and (C). You will hear the statements or questions, as well as the responses, just one time and they are not printed in your test booklet. Therefore, you must listen very carefully. Select the best response and fill in the corresponding oval on your answer sheet. You will have 15 seconds to answer each question.

Question 1   (A)   (B)   (C)

Question 2   (A)   (B)   (C)

Question 3   (A)   (B)   (C)

Question 4   (A)   (B)   (C)

Question 5   (A)   (B)   (C)

Question 6   (A)   (B)   (C)

Question 7   (A)   (B)   (C)

Question 8   (A)   (B)   (C)

Question 9   (A)   (B)   (C)

Question 10   (A)   (B)   (C)

Question 11   (A)   (B)   (C)

Question 12   (A)   (B)   (C)

Question 13   (A)   (B)   (C)

Question 14   (A)   (B)   (C)

Question 15   (A)   (B)   (C)

Part B

Directions: You will now hear a series of short selections. You will hear them only once and they are not printed in your test booklet. After each selection, you will be asked one or more questions about what you have just heard. These questions, with four possible answers, are printed in your test booklet. Select the best answer to each question from among the four choices given and fill in the corresponding oval on your answer sheet. You will have 15 seconds to answer each question.

Question 16   What are they competing for?

    (A)   putting on costumes

    (B)   playing firecrackers

    (C)   decorating houses

    (D)   blowing up balloons

Question 17   What does she usually do at home?

    (A)   watches TV

    (B)   plays cards

    (C)   plays on the computer

    (D)   exercises

Question 18   Which department does she wants to see?

    (A)   internal medicine

    (B)   radiology

    (C)   neurology

    (D)   gynecology

Question 19   What did he have for lunch?

    (A)   fried rice

    (B)   dumplings

    (C)   noodle

    (D)   bread

Question 20   Where does the girl want to go?

    (A)   Bejing

    (B)   Taipei

    (C)   Tokyo

    (D)   France

Question 21   What kind of fruits does the girl like?

    (A)   banana and plum

    (B)   banana and apple

    (C)   everything besides banana and plum

    (D)   anything, especially banana and plum

Question 22   Which floor should they go to find the shoes?

    (A)   first floor

    (B)   second floor

    (C)   third floor

    (D)   fourth floor

Question 23   Whom is she talking to?

    (A)   a teacher

    (B)   a hair stylist

    (C)   a child

    (D)   a doctor

Question 24   How is he planning on moving?

    (A)   He is going to rent a moving van and move on his own.

    (B)   He is going to hire a moving company.

    (C)   He has not decided yet.

    (D)   He has not decided whether to move or not.

Question 25   What type of job does the woman have?

    (A)   gardener

    (B)   teacher

    (C)   librarian

    (D)   babysitter

Question 26 Which of the following activities they may do on Saturday?

(A) go to the movies

(B) go hiking

(C) go camping

(D) go biking

Question 27 What could this place be?

(A) a home

(B) a hospital

(C) a vet hospital

(D) a department store

Question 28 What school are they attending?

(A) college

(B) high school

(C) middle school

(D) language school

Question 29 How many people are actually going to the movie?

(A) 6 people

(B) 5 people

(C) 4 people

(D) 3 people

Question 30 What lesson does the girl not take?

(A) history

(B) Japanese

(C) Latin

(D) chemistry

SAT II 中文模擬試題 第六套
Section I : Listening Comprehension

Part A

Directions: In this part of the test you will hear short questions, statements, or exchanges in Mandarin Chinese, followed by three responses designated (A), (B), and (C). You will hear the statements or questions, as well as the responses, just one time and they are not printed in your test booklet. Therefore, you must listen very carefully. Select the best response and fill in the corresponding oval on your answer sheet. You will have 15 seconds to answer each question.

Question 1

紐約的911恐怖事件對整個美國的安全系統是一個挑戰。

    (A) 所以現在快打911電話求救。

    (B) 所以現在沒有安全系統了。

    (C) 所以現在搭飛機檢查比以前仔細和嚴格多了。

Question 2

您打那兒來？

    (A) 我打一兒去。

    (B) 我不打電話。

    (C) 中國。

Question 3

這間廟裏面有很多人呢！

    (A) 是啊，和尚正在唸經呢！

    (B) 是啊，神父正在布施！

    (C) 是啊，牧師正在講道！

Question 4

能不能麻煩你開車送我去圖書館？

    (A) 不好意思。

    (B) 太可惜。

    (C) 沒問題。

Question 5

最近我們要期末考，每天忙得我都不知道東南西北了。

    (A) 他不喜歡考試。

    (B) 他很忙。

    (C) 他對方向不清楚。

Question 6

昨天晚上我去聽音樂會，王小明也去了。

    (A) 只有王小明去。

    (B) 我們誰都沒去。

    (C) 我和王小明都去了。

Question 7

週末你都做些什麼？

    (A) 我是個畫家。

    (B) 上個週末，我去了紐約一趟剛回來。

    (C) 看看書、做做運動，如此而已。

Question 8

這學期你選修幾門課？

    (A) 除了英文、數學還有木工。

    (B) 我已經請人來修門了。

    (C) 剛考完期中考，可以休息幾天。

Question 9

你的背包裏裝了什麼東西？

    (A) 我要把書架裝起來。

    (B) 我的背部很痛。

    (C) 都是飲料，才會這麼重。

Question 10

你會不會錯過下一班車？

    (A) 我看錯了車牌。

    (B) 我停錯地方了。

    (C) 不會，還有半個小時。

Question 11

你買菜時，順便幫我買份報紙，好嗎？

    (A) 我看了今天的報紙。

    (B) 沒問題。

    (C) 我還不知道買什麼菜。

Question 12

從這裏到郵局怎麼走？

    (A) 我們走路去郵局。

    (B) 我要買一些郵票。

    (C) 前面那條路右轉就可以看到。

Question 13

他的年紀雖然小，可是小提琴拉得很不錯。

    (A) 錯了！他不是在拉小提琴。

    (B) 他彈錯了好幾個音。

    (C) 是啊！他已經得過好幾個獎。

Question 14

我不知道買些什麼化妝品送她？

    (A) 你可以買口紅。

    (B) 她每天都會用化妝品。

    (C) 化妝品很貴。

Question 15

不好意思，還讓你親自送來。

    (A) 我不明白你的意思。

    (B) 沒關係，我順路。

    (C) 把你的意思告訴我。

Part B

Directions: You will now hear a series of short selections. You will hear them <u>only once</u> and they are not printed in your test booklet. After each selection, you will be asked one or more questions about what you have just heard. These questions, with four possible answers, are printed in your test booklet. Select the best answer to each question from among the four choices given and fill in the corresponding oval on your answer sheet. You will have 15 seconds to answer each question.

Question 16

男：萬聖節要怎麼過？

女：打扮得怪模怪樣的，去鄰居家要糖。

男：我可以替弟弟打扮，讓他化裝成吸血鬼。

女：我要幫妹妹扮成巫婆。

男：好，看我們誰的化裝技術好。

Question 17

男：王玲，你平常在家裏，怎麼打發日子的？

女：我沒事就盯著電視看。

男：別老坐著不動，應該出去走走，運動運動。

女：好，明天我就跟你一塊兒去打網球吧！

Question 18

男：玲達！你怎麼也到醫院來了？

女：是啊，我來看病的。

男：你要看那一科呢？

女：我要看內科。

Question 19

女：你中午吃些什麼？

男：我去一家餐廳，想吃餃子，可是要等半個小時，想吃包子又沒有，最後只好叫了一盤炒飯。

Question 20

女：我想買一張七月初到東京的來回機票。

男：有的航空公司要一千多塊，有的不到一千。

女：哪家的便宜，就買哪家的。

男：韓國航空公司的票最便宜，不過要轉兩次機。

女：這太麻煩了，我還是坐直飛的好了。

Question 21

男：女生都喜歡吃水果，我想你也不例外。

女：除了香蕉和李子，我沒有不喜歡的。

Question 22

男：我們這兒一樓賣化妝品，二樓賣服裝和鞋帽，三樓賣家電用品，請問你們想買什麼？

女：我們想看一看小孩子的衣服。

Question 23

女：老板，我的頭髮需要剪短一點，同時也要燙一下。

男：今天人很多，你要再等一個多鐘頭。

女：那我改天再來。

Question 24

女：你什麼時候搬家？

男：下星期三。

女：你跟搬家公司聯絡好了嗎？

男：我打算租輛小貨車自己搬。

Question 25

女：我第一次當保姆，沒有經驗。

男：只要有耐心，講些故事，陪他們玩就好了。

女：請問多少錢一小時？

男：我付你一小時八塊錢。

Question 26

女：星期六我們去爬山或是去露營，好嗎？

男：氣象報告說星期六會下大雨，這種天氣我看不如在家裏看電視好了。

女：看電影總可以吧？

男：可以，就是不要戶外活動。

Question 27

男：小姐，你的狼狗已經好多了。

女：太好了。

男：牠今天可以回家了。

女：謝謝醫生。

Question 28

男：現在的高中課程裏，你比較喜歡的科目是什麼？

女：我喜歡歷史和文學，你呢？

男：我比較喜歡物理和化學。

女：我們倆喜歡的可真是不同啊！一個理科，一個文科。

Question 29

女：我約了五個同學和我一起去看四點的電影。

男：快三點了，他們都來了嗎？

女：有一個剛打電話說不能來，其他的人都來了。

Question 30

男：下學期你選了哪些課？

女：下學期我選了英文、數學、歷史、拉丁文、化學和一堂體育課。

SAT II 中文模擬試題 第六套
Section II : Grammar

Directions: This section consists of a number of incomplete statements, each of which has four suggested completions. Select the word or phrase that best completes the sentence structurally and logically. Please fill in the corresponding oval on the answer sheet.

THE QUESTIONS ARE PRESENTED IN FOUR DIFFERENT WRITING SYSTEMS: TRADITIONAL CHARACTERS, SIMPLIFIED CHARACTERS, PINYIN ROMANIZATION, AND CHINESE PHONETIC ALPHABET(BO PO MO FO). TO SAVE TIME, IT IS RECOMMENDED THAT YOU CHOOSE THE WRITING SYSTEM WITH WHICH YOU ARE MOST FAMILIAR WITH AND **READ ONLY THAT VERSION OF THE QUESTION.**

31. _____由你，柯林頓的公司裏，300
位員工全是女性。

    (A) 要不要

    (B) 信不信

    (C) 想不想

    (D) 有沒有

31. _____由你，柯林頓的公司里，300
位員工全是女性。

    (A) 要不要

    (B) 信不信

    (C) 想不想

    (D) 有沒有

31. _____ ㄧㄡˊ ㄋㄧˇ，ㄎㄜ ㄌㄧㄣˊ ㄉㄨㄣˋ ㄉㄜ˙ ㄍㄨㄥ ㄙ ㄌㄧˇ，300
ㄨㄟˋ ㄩㄢˊ ㄍㄨㄥ ㄑㄩㄢˊ ㄕˋ ㄋㄩˇ ㄒㄧㄥˋ。

    (A) ㄧㄠˋ ㄅㄨˊ ㄧㄠˋ

    (B) ㄒㄧㄣˋ ㄅㄨˊ ㄒㄧㄣˋ

    (C) ㄒㄧㄤˇ ㄅㄨˋ ㄒㄧㄤˇ

    (D) ㄧㄡˇ ㄇㄟˊ ㄧㄡˇ

31. _____ yóu nǐ, Kelíndùn de gōng sī lǐ, 300 wèi
yuán gōng quán shì nǔ xìng.

    (A) Yào bú yào

    (B) Xìn bú xìn

    (C) Xiǎng bù xiǎng

    (D) Yǒu méi yǒu

32. _____美國的經濟情況不好，很多公
司都在裁員。

    (A) 於是

    (B) 由來

    (C) 由於

    (D) 有沒有

32. _____美国的经济情况不好，很多公
司都在裁员。

    (A) 于是

    (B) 由来

    (C) 由于

    (D) 有沒有

32. _____ ㄇㄟˇ ㄍㄨㄛˊ ㄉㄜ˙ ㄐㄧㄥ ㄐㄧˋ ㄑㄧㄥˊ ㄎㄨㄤˋ ㄅㄨˋ ㄏㄠˇ，ㄏㄣˇ ㄉㄨㄛ ㄍㄨㄥ ㄙ
ㄉㄡ ㄗㄞˋ ㄘㄞˊ ㄩㄢˊ。

    (A) ㄩˊ ㄕˋ

    (B) ㄧㄡˊ ㄌㄞˊ

    (C) ㄧㄡˊ ㄩˊ

    (D) ㄧㄡˇ ㄇㄟˊ ㄧㄡˇ

32. _____ Měiguó de jīng jì qíng kuàng bù hǎo,
hěn duō gōng sī dōu zài cái yuán.

    (A) Yú shì

    (B) Yóu lái

    (C) Yóu yú

    (D) Yǒu méi yǒu

33. 他上課 ___ 說話，___ 老師不喜歡他。

   (A) 一邊…一邊

   (B) 不是…就是

   (C) 總是…難怪

   (D) 有時…有時

33. 他上课 ___ 说话，___ 老师不喜欢他。

   (A) 一边…一边

   (B) 不是…就是

   (C) 总是…难怪

   (D) 有时…有时

33. Tā shàng kè ___ shuō huà, ___ lǎo shī bù xǐ huān tā.

   (A) yì biān .... yì biān

   (B) bú shì .... jiù shì

   (C) zǒng shì .... nán guài

   (D) yǒu shí .... yǒu shí

34. 她 ___ 聰明，___ 不會開車。

   (A) 如此…竟然

   (B) 除了…以外

   (C) 因為…所以

   (D) 當然…可以

34. 她 ___ 聪明，___ 不会开车。

   (A) 如此…竟然

   (B) 除了…以外

   (C) 因为…所以

   (D) 当然…可以

34. Tā ___ cōng míng, ___ bú huì kāi chē?

   (A) rú cǐ .... jìng rán

   (B) chú le .... yǐ wài

   (C) yīn wèi .... suǒ yǐ

   (D) dāng rán .... kě yǐ

35. 這道理實在是難了一點兒，___，
難不倒我！

   (A) 不過

   (B) 還要

   (C) 不久

   (D) 不是

35. 这道理实在是难了一点儿，___，
难不倒我！

   (A) 不过

   (B) 还要

   (C) 不久

   (D) 不是

35. Zhè dào lǐ shí zài shì nán le yì diǎnr, ___ ,
nán bù dǎo wǒ!

   (A) bú guò

   (B) hái yào

   (C) bù jiǔ

   (D) bú shì

36. 小妹太累了，____ 她站著也能睡。
(A) 沒想到
(B) 看不到
(C) 辦不到
(D) 想到

36. 小妹太累了，____ 她站著也能睡。
(A) 没想到
(B) 看不到
(C) 办不到
(D) 想到

36. ㄒㄠ ㄇㄟ ㄊㄞ ㄌㄟ ˙ㄌㄜ，____ ㄊㄚ ㄓㄢ ˙ㄓㄜ ㄧㄝ ㄋㄥ ㄕㄟ 。
(A) ㄇㄟ ㄒㄤ ㄉㄠ
(B) ㄎㄢ ㄅㄨ ㄉㄠ
(C) ㄅㄢ ㄅㄨ ㄉㄠ
(D) ㄒㄤ ㄉㄠ

36. Xiǎo mèi tài lèi le, ____ tā zhàn zhe yě néng shuì.
(A) méi xiǎng dào
(B) kàn bú dào
(C) bàn bú dào
(D) xiǎng dào

---

37. 學校 ____ 開學三個月了。
(A) 曾經
(B) 已經
(C) 經過
(D) 剛才

37. 学校 ____ 开学三个月了。
(A) 曾经
(B) 已经
(C) 经过
(D) 刚才

37. ㄒㄩㄝ ㄒㄠ ____ ㄎㄞ ㄒㄩㄝ ㄙㄢ ˙ㄍㄜ ㄩㄝ ˙ㄌㄜ 。
(A) ㄘㄥ ㄐㄧㄥ
(B) ㄧ ㄐㄧㄥ
(C) ㄐㄧㄥ ㄍㄨㄛ
(D) ㄍㄤ ㄘㄞ

37. Xué xiào ____ kāi xué sān ge yuè le.
(A) céng jīng
(B) yǐ jīng
(C) jīng guò
(D) gāng cái

---

38. ____ 因爲今年911事件，我早就去華盛頓參觀了。
(A) 自從
(B) 還是
(C) 是不是
(D) 要不是

38. ____ 因爲今年911事件，我早就去华盛顿参观了。
(A) 自从
(B) 还是
(C) 是不是
(D) 要不是

38. ____ ㄧㄣ ㄨㄟ ㄐㄧㄣ ㄋㄧㄢ 911 ㄕ ㄐㄧㄢ，ㄨㄛ ㄗㄠ ㄐㄧㄡ ㄑㄩ ㄏㄨㄚ ㄕㄥ ㄉㄨㄣ ㄘㄢ ㄍㄨㄢ ˙ㄌㄜ 。
(A) ㄗ ㄘㄨㄥ
(B) ㄏㄞ ㄕ
(C) ㄕ ㄅㄨ ㄕ
(D) ㄧㄠ ㄅㄨ ㄕ

38. ____ yīn wèi jīn nián 911 shì jiàn, wǒ zǎo jiù qù Huáshèngdùn cān guān le.
(A) Zì cóng
(B) Hái shì
(C) Shì bú shì
(D) Yào bú shì

39. 不管世貿中心有沒有被炸掉，___我都要去紐約。

    (A) 反正

    (B) 反而

    (C) 而是

    (D) 一定

39. 不管世贸中心有没有被炸掉，___我都要去纽约。

    (A) 反正

    (B) 反而

    (C) 而是

    (D) 一定

39. ㄅㄨˋ ㄍㄨㄢˇ ㄕˋ ㄇㄠˋ ㄓㄨㄥ ㄒㄧㄣ ㄧㄡˇ ㄇㄟˊ ㄧㄡˇ ㄅㄟˋ ㄓㄚˋ ㄉㄧㄠˋ，___ ㄨㄛˇ ㄉㄡ ㄧㄠˋ ㄑㄩˋ ㄋㄧㄡˇ ㄩㄝ。

    (A) ㄈㄢˇ ㄓㄥˋ

    (B) ㄈㄢˇ ㄦˊ

    (C) ㄦˊ ㄕˋ

    (D) ㄧˊ ㄉㄧㄥˋ

39. Bù guǎn shì mào zhōng xīn yǒu méi yǒu bèi zhà diào, ____ wǒ dōu yào qù Niǔyuē.

    (A) fǎn zhèng

    (B) fǎn ér

    (C) ér shì

    (D) yí dìng

---

40. 他不但不改過，____ 越來越壞。

    (A) 反正

    (B) 可是

    (C) 即使

    (D) 反而

40. 他不但不改过，____ 越来越坏。

    (A) 反正

    (B) 可是

    (C) 即使

    (D) 反而

40. ㄊㄚ ㄅㄨˊ ㄉㄢˋ ㄅㄨˋ ㄍㄞˇ ㄍㄨㄛˋ，____ ㄩㄝˋ ㄌㄞˊ ㄩㄝˋ ㄏㄨㄞˋ。

    (A) ㄈㄢˇ ㄓㄥˋ

    (B) ㄎㄜˇ ㄕˋ

    (C) ㄐㄧˊ ㄕˇ

    (D) ㄈㄢˇ ㄦˊ

40. Tā bú dàn bù gǎi guò, ____ yuè lái yuè huài.

    (A) fǎn zhèng

    (B) kě shì

    (C) jí shǐ

    (D) fǎn ér

---

41. 我去書店買了____ 報紙。

    (A) 一張

    (B) 一把

    (C) 一份

    (D) 一堆

41. 我去书店买了____ 报纸。

    (A) 一张

    (B) 一把

    (C) 一分

    (D) 一堆

41. ㄨㄛˇ ㄑㄩˋ ㄕㄨ ㄉㄧㄢˋ ㄇㄞˇ ㄌㄜ ____ ㄅㄠˋ ㄓˇ。

    (A) ㄧ ㄓㄤ

    (B) ㄧ ㄅㄚˇ

    (C) ㄧ ㄈㄣˋ

    (D) ㄧ ㄉㄨㄟ

41. Wǒ qù shū diàn mǎi le ____ bào zhǐ.

    (A) yì zhāng

    (B) yì bǎ

    (C) yí fèn

    (D) yì duī

42. 差一刻六點，是 _____ 。

    (A) 5:45

    (B) 5:59

    (C) 6:15

    (D) 5:15

42. ㄔ ㄧ ㄎㄜ ㄌㄧㄡ ㄉㄧㄢ，ㄕ _____ 。

    (A) 5:45

    (B) 5:59

    (C) 6:15

    (D) 5:15

42. 差一刻六点，是 _____ 。

    (A) 5:45

    (B) 5:59

    (C) 6:15

    (D) 5:15

42. Chā yí kè liù diǎn, shì _____ .

    (A) 5:45

    (B) 5:59

    (C) 6:15

    (D) 5:15

---

43. 最近天氣 _____ ，很容易生病。

    (A) 不冷不熱

    (B) 很冷很熱

    (C) 忽冷不熱

    (D) 忽冷忽熱

43. ㄗㄨㄟ ㄐㄧㄣ ㄊㄧㄢ ㄑㄧ _____ ，ㄏㄣ ㄖㄨㄥ ㄧ ㄕㄥ ㄅㄧㄥ 。

    (A) ㄅㄨ ㄌㄥ ㄅㄨ ㄖㄜ

    (B) ㄏㄣ ㄌㄥ ㄏㄣ ㄖㄜ

    (C) ㄏㄨ ㄌㄥ ㄅㄨ ㄖㄜ

    (D) ㄏㄨ ㄌㄥ ㄏㄨ ㄖㄜ

43. 最近天气 _____ ，很容易生病。

    (A) 不冷不热

    (B) 很冷很热

    (C) 忽冷不热

    (D) 忽冷忽热

43. Zuì jìn tiān qì _____ , hěn róng yì shēng bìng.

    (A) bù lěng bú rè

    (B) hěn lěng hěn rè

    (C) hū lěng bú rè

    (D) hū lěng hū rè

---

44. 表妹雖然在美國長大，但是說了 _____ 流利的中文。

    (A) 一口

    (B) 一把

    (C) 一篇

    (D) 一段

44. ㄅㄧㄠ ㄇㄟ ㄙㄨㄟ ㄖㄢ ㄗㄞ ㄇㄟ ㄍㄨㄛ ㄓㄤ ㄉㄚ，ㄉㄢ ㄕ ㄕㄨㄛ ㄌㄜ _____ ㄌㄧㄡ ㄌㄧ ㄉㄜ ㄓㄨㄥ ㄨㄣ 。

    (A) ㄧ ㄎㄡ

    (B) ㄧ ㄅㄚ

    (C) ㄧ ㄆㄧㄢ

    (D) ㄧ ㄉㄨㄢ

44. 表妹虽然在美国长大，但是说了 _____ 流利的中文。

    (A) 一口

    (B) 一把

    (C) 一篇

    (D) 一段

44. Biǎo mèi suī rán zài Měiguó zhǎng dà, dàn shì shuō le _____ liú lì de Zhōngwén.

    (A) yì kǒu

    (B) yì bǎ

    (C) yì piān

    (D) yí duàn

45. ＿＿你不打球，＿＿我們可以一塊兒練習。

    (A) 因爲…所以

    (B) 可惜…否則

    (C) 雖然…所以

    (D) 雖然…如此

45. ＿＿你不打球，＿＿我们可以一块儿练习。

    (A) 因为…所以

    (B) 可惜…否则

    (C) 虽然…所以

    (D) 虽然…如此

45. ＿＿ nǐ bù dǎ qiú, ＿＿ wǒ men kě yǐ yí kuàir liàn xí.

    (A) Yīn wèi …. suǒ yǐ

    (B) Kě xí …. fǒu zé

    (C) Suī rán …. suǒ yǐ

    (D) Suī rán …. rú cǐ

46. 我們的旅程是從洛衫機 ＿＿ 到三藩市。

    (A) 西行

    (B) 南下

    (C) 東行

    (D) 北上

46. 我们的旅程是从洛衫机 ＿＿ 到三藩市。

    (A) 西行

    (B) 南下

    (C) 东行

    (D) 北上

46. Wǒ men de lǚ chéng shì cóng Luòshānjī ＿＿ dào Sānfánshì.

    (A) xī xíng

    (B) nán xià

    (C) dōng xíng

    (D) běi shàng

47. 說話沒有禮貌，很容易＿＿別人。

    (A) 尊重

    (B) 得罪

    (C) 得到

    (D) 得失

47. 说话没有礼貌，很容易＿＿别人。

    (A) 尊重

    (B) 得罪

    (C) 得到

    (D) 得失

47. Shuō huà méi yǒu lǐ mào, hěn róng yì ＿＿ bié rén.

    (A) zūn zhòng

    (B) dé zuì

    (C) dé dào

    (D) dé shī

48. 妹妹＿＿可愛，＿＿聰明，大家都很喜歡她。

    (A) 也…也

    (B) 既…又

    (C) 一邊…一邊

    (D) 一會兒…一會兒

48. ㄇㄟˋ ㄇㄟ ＿＿ㄎㄜˇ ㄞˋ，＿＿ㄘㄨㄥ ㄇㄧㄥˊ，ㄉㄚˋ ㄐㄧㄚ ㄉㄡ ㄏㄣˇ ㄒㄧˇ ㄏㄨㄢ ㄊㄚ。

    (A) ㄧㄝˇ … ㄧㄝˇ

    (B) ㄐㄧˋ … ㄧㄡˋ

    (C) ㄧ ㄅㄧㄢ … ㄧ ㄅㄧㄢ

    (D) ㄧ ㄏㄨㄟˇ ㄦ … ㄧ ㄏㄨㄟˇ ㄦ

48. 妹妹＿＿可愛，＿＿聪明，大家都很喜欢她。

    (A) 也…也

    (B) 既…又

    (C) 一边…一边

    (D) 一会儿…一会儿

48. Mèi mei ＿＿ kě ài, ＿＿cōng míng, dà jiā dōu hěn xǐ huān tā.

    (A) yě .... yě

    (B) jì .... yòu

    (C) yì biān .... yì biān

    (D) yì huǐr .... yì huǐr

49. 要＿＿才能算是個健康的人呢？

    (A) 那麼樣

    (B) 什麼樣

    (C) 這麼樣

    (D) 怎麼樣

49. ㄧㄠˋ＿＿ㄘㄞˊ ㄋㄥˊ ㄙㄨㄢˋ ㄕˋ ㄍㄜˋ ㄐㄧㄢˋ ㄎㄤ ㄉㄜ˙ ㄖㄣˊ ㄋㄜ˙？

    (A) ㄋㄚˋ ㄇㄜ˙ ㄧㄤˋ

    (B) ㄕㄣˊ ㄇㄜ˙ ㄧㄤˋ

    (C) ㄓㄜˋ ㄇㄜ˙ ㄧㄤˋ

    (D) ㄗㄣˇ ㄇㄜ˙ ㄧㄤˋ

49. 要＿＿才能算是个健康的人呢？

    (A) 那么样

    (B) 什么样

    (C) 这么样

    (D) 怎么样

49. Yào ＿＿ cái néng suàn shì ge jiàn kāng de rén ne?

    (A) nà me yàng

    (B) shén me yàng

    (C) zhè me yàng

    (D) zěn me yàng

50. 只要肯努力，成功的大門就在＿＿。

    (A) 之前

    (B) 門前

    (C) 眼前

    (D) 以前

50. ㄓˇ ㄧㄠˋ ㄎㄣˇ ㄋㄨˇ ㄌㄧˋ，ㄔㄥˊ ㄍㄨㄥ ㄉㄜ˙ ㄉㄚˋ ㄇㄣˊ ㄐㄧㄡˋ ㄗㄞˋ ＿＿。

    (A) ㄓ ㄑㄧㄢˊ

    (B) ㄇㄣˊ ㄑㄧㄢˊ

    (C) ㄧㄢˇ ㄑㄧㄢˊ

    (D) ㄧˇ ㄑㄧㄢˊ

50. 只要肯努力，成功的大门就在＿＿。

    (A) 之前

    (B) 门前

    (C) 眼前

    (D) 以前

50. Zhǐ yào kěn nǔ lì, chéng gōng de dà mén jiù zài ＿＿ .

    (A) zhī qián

    (B) mén qián

    (C) yǎn qián

    (D) yǐ qián

51. 這麼難寫的字，＿＿是你了，＿＿我都不會寫。

    (A) 不光…只有

    (B) 不只…還

    (C) 別說…連

    (D) 不但…也

51. 这么难写的字，＿＿是你了，＿＿我都不会写。

    (A) 不光…只有

    (B) 不只…还

    (C) 别说…连

    (D) 不但…也

51. Zhè me nán xiě de zì, ＿＿ shì nǐ le, ＿＿ wǒ dōu bú huì xiě.

    (A) bù guāng .... zhǐ yǒu

    (B) bù zhǐ .... hái

    (C) bié shuō .... lián

    (D) bú dàn .... yě

52. 他雖然生病，精神＿＿很好。

    (A) 都

    (B) 卻

    (C) 多

    (D) 但

52. 他虽然生病，精神＿＿很好。

    (A) 都

    (B) 却

    (C) 多

    (D) 但

52. Tā suī rán shēng bìng, jīng shén ＿＿ hěn hǎo.

    (A) dōu

    (B) què

    (C) duō

    (D) dàn

53. 這雙鞋＿＿十塊錢＿＿能買到。

    (A) 只是…才

    (B) 只能…就

    (C) 只要…就

    (D) 只好…才

53. 这双鞋＿＿十块钱＿＿能买到。

    (A) 只是…才

    (B) 只能…就

    (C) 只要…就

    (D) 只好…才

53. Zhè shuāng xié ＿＿shí kuài qián ＿＿néng mǎi dào .

    (A) zhǐ shì .... cái

    (B) zhǐ néng .... jiù

    (C) zhǐ yào .... jiù

    (D) zhǐ hǎo .... cái

54. 下雨天＿＿能出去玩，＿＿得關在家裏，真苦惱。

    (A) 不但…而且

    (B) 不光…又

    (C) 不只…還

    (D) 不但不…反而

54. 下雨天＿＿能出去玩，＿＿得关在家里，真苦恼。

    (A) 不但…而且

    (B) 不光…又

    (C) 不只…還

    (D) 不但不…反而

54. Xià yǔ tiān ＿＿ néng chū qù wán, ＿＿ děi guān zài jiā lǐ, zhēn kǔ nǎo.

    (A) bú dàn .... ér qiě

    (B) bù guāng ....yòu

    (C) bù zhǐ .... hái

    (D) bú dàn bù .... fǎn ér

---

55. 時間像流水，過去了就＿＿回頭。

    (A) 不但

    (B) 不想

    (C) 不要

    (D) 不再

55. 时间像流水，过去了就＿＿回头。

    (A) 不但

    (B) 不想

    (C) 不要

    (D) 不再

55. Shí jiān xiàng liú shuǐ, guò qù le jiù ＿＿ huí tóu.

    (A) bú dàn

    (B) bù xiǎng

    (C) bú yào

    (D) bú zài

SAT II 中文模擬試題 第六套
Section III : Reading Comprehension

Directions: Read the following selections carefully for comprehension. Each selection is followed by one or more questions or incomplete statements based on its content. Select the answer or completion that is best according to the passage and fill in the corresponding oval on the answer sheet.

THIS SECTION OF THE TEST IS PRESENTED IN TWO WRITING SYSTEMS: TRADITIONAL CHARACTERS AND SIMPLIFIED CHARACTERS. IT IS RECOMMENDED THAT YOU CHOOSE <u>ONLY</u> THAT WRITING SYSTEM WITH WHICH YOU ARE MOST FAMILIAR AS YOU WORK THROUGH THIS SECTION OF THE TEST.

56~57

母親節海鮮大餐

10:30 am - 2:30 pm

母親節牛排晚餐

4:00 pm -9:00 pm

母亲节海鲜大餐

10:30 am - 2:30 pm

母亲节牛排晚餐

4:00 pm -9:00 pm

Question 56   What special event is this ad for?

(A)   Chinese New Year

(B)   Father's Day

(C)   Mother's Day

(D)   Teacher's Day

Question 57   If my special guest likes to have seafood for meal, we should be at the restaurant no later than-

(A)   10:30 am

(B)   2:30 pm

(C)   4:00 pm

(D)   9:00 pm

58~59

孔子说三人行必有我<u>师</u>

孔子说三人行必有我师

Question 58　　Whose statement is it?

(A)　　Mr. Meng

(B)　　son of Mr. Kong

(C)　　an old man

(D)　　Confucius

Question 59　　The underlined phrase most nearly means?

(A)　　teacher

(B)　　friend

(C)　　enemy

(D)　　student

60

1. 中國童話故事書（第一冊）
2. 中國童話故事書（第二冊）
3. 中國童話故事書（第三冊）
4. 中國童話故事書（第四冊）
　　以上每冊定價一百元
5. 中國童話故事書全集（一套共四冊）
　　特價三百五十元

1. 中国童话故事书（第一册）
2. 中国童话故事书（第二册）
3. 中国童话故事书（第三册）
4. 中国童话故事书（第四册）
　　以上每册定价一百元
5. 中国童话故事书全集（一套共四册）
　　特价三百五十元

Question 60　　How much would you pay if you want to buy a set of Chinese fairy tale books?

(A)　　100.00 dollars

(B)　　400.00 dollars

(C)　　350.00 dollars

(D)　　300.00 dollars

61

大套房出租
Cupertino 近天天超市
簡單傢俱獨立電話線
出入方便月租 $590 包水電
限單身不吸煙正職人士
(408) 930-6892

大套房出租
Cupertino近天天超市
简单傢俱独立电话线
出入方便月租 $590 包水电
限单身不吸烟正职人士
(408) 930-6892

Question 61   This ad is for

    (A)   selling a car

    (B)   selling a house

    (C)   renting a room

    (D)   renting a car

62~63

歲末大拍賣
全面七折起

岁末大拍卖
全面七折起

Question 62   When will this sale be happening?

    (A)   summer

    (B)   Thanksgiving holiday

    (C)   year-end holiday

    (D)   spring

Question 63   What is the minimum discount?

    (A)   70% off

    (B)   30% off

    (C)   50% off

    (D)   35% off

64

時代快速變化

人們變得壓抑和沉重

需要交流和溝通來抒解壓力

新生代-上網聊天

老生代-促膝談心

时代快速变化

人们变得压抑和沉重

需要交流和沟通来抒解压力

新生代-上网聊天

老生代-促膝谈心

Question 64　　　According to the article, _____ is a way to reduce stress.

(A) joining the army

(B) playing computer games

(C) attending church

(D) communicating with others

65~67

京劇晚會

京劇是中國民族文化的瑰寶

想瞭解中國嗎？

請來欣賞京劇

本週六晚七點

本校禮堂

京剧晚会

京剧是中国民族文化的瑰宝

想了解中国吗？

请来欣赏京剧

本週六晚七点

本校礼堂

Question 65　　　This is an advertisement for _____

(A) the Guangdong Opera

(B) the Beijing Opera

(C) a concert

(D) a magic show

Question 66　　　Where is the location?

(A) cafeteria

(B) Beijing Opera

(C) auditorium

(D) campus

Question 67   When is the show time?

    (A)   this Saturday at 7:00 pm

    (B)   this Saturday at 7:00 am

    (C)   next Saturday at 7:00 pm

    (D)   next Saturday at 7:00 am

 # 68

男賓止步	男宾止步

Question 68   What does this sign mean?

    (A)   female visitors only

    (B)   emergency exit

    (C)   information desk

    (D)   male visitors only

 # 69~70

每個星期六，我都得開二十分鐘的車去上法文課，每次上兩個小時，每週一次，再上三個月，我就要放假了。	每个星期六，我都得开二十分钟的车去上法文课，每次上两个小时，每周一次，再上三个月，我就要放假了。

Question 69   What class am I taking currently?

    (A)   law school

    (B)   German language class

    (C)   grammar school

    (D)   French language class

Question 70   How often do I have to go to the class?

    (A)   everyday

    (B)   once a week

    (C)   twice a week

    (D)   three times a month

從 2000年七月至 2001年六月間，共有一百九十二個國家、四十萬名學生參加托福測驗，平均分數是535分。

臺灣學生共有三萬四千多人報名，人數僅次於日本、中國、南韓、印度，平均分數只有五百一十五分，遠低於印度的五百八十一分、菲律賓的五百六十五分、中國的五百九十分及南韓的五百三十三分，但高於日本。

从 2000年七月至 2001年六月间，共有一百九十二个国家、四十万名学生参加托福测验，平均分数是535分。

台湾学生共有三万四千多人报名，人数仅次於日本、中国、南韩、印度，平均分数只有五百一十五分，远低於印度的五百八十一分、菲律宾的五百六十五分、中国的五百九十分及南韩的五百三十三分，但高於日本。

Question 71 What is the average test score of students from India?

(A) 535

(B) 581

(C) 515

(D) 565

Question 72 According to this article which nation has the highest average test score?

(A) India

(B) Japan

(C) China

(D) South Korea

Question 73 According to this article which nation has the lowest average test score?

(A) Japan

(B) Korea

(C) Taiwan

(D) The Philippines

74

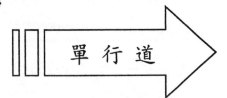 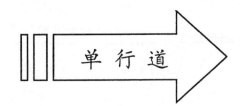

Question 74   What does this sign mean?

(A)   One lane

(B)   Pedestrians only

(C)   One-way street

(D)   No U-turn

75~77

出生於1946年到1964年的嬰兒潮
世代占全美的三分之一人口，
特色是擁有良好的教育，四分
之一的人有大學以上的學歷，
四分之三的人擁有自宅，平均
年收入有十萬元。

出生於1946年到1964年的嬰兒潮
世代占全美的三分之一人口，
特色是擁有良好的教育，四分
之一的人有大学以上的学历，
四分之三的人拥有自宅，平均
年收入有十万元。

Question 75   According to this paragraph, the baby-boom generation is _____ of the population?

(A)   2/3

(B)   1/4

(C)   3/4

(D)   1/3

Question 76   What is the average annual income of this generation?

(A) $1,000,000.00

(B) $200,000.00

(C) $100,000.00

(D) $110,000.00

Question 77   What is the percentage of baby-boomer generation are home owners?

    (A)   25%

    (B)   75%

    (C)   35%

    (D)   33%

 # 78~79

【華人素描】	
華人多久檢查一次身體？	
一些保險公司爲減少開支，限制醫生就診病人時間，促使市面上自我診斷書刊的蓬勃。	
未曾	24.8%
半年之內	3.8%
半年一次	8%
一年一次	42.3%
半年兩次	6.6%
半年多於兩次	3.3%
不知道	10.3%

【华人素描】	
华人多久检查一次身体？	
一些保险公司为减少开支，限制医生就诊病人时间，促使市面上自我诊断书刊的蓬勃。	
未曾	24.8%
半年之内	3.8%
半年一次	8%
一年一次	42.3%
半年两次	6.6%
半年多于两次	3.3%
不知道	10.3%

Question 78   How often do the majority of Chinese people go in for a physical check up?

    (A)   once every 6 months

    (B)   once every year

    (C)   once every other year

    (D)   never

Question 79   What percentage of interviewees have a check up more than twice every half year?

    (A)   3.8%

    (B)   6.6%

    (C)   3.3%

    (D)   8%

80

把握最後機會
出清所有月曆

全面半價

自 $2 起
售完爲止、先到先得

把握最后机会
出清所有月历

全面半价

自 $2 起
售完为止、先到先得

Question 80

What is the ad promoting?

(A) calendars

(B) clothes

(C) used cars

(D) old furniture

81~82

十月十七日 　 星期四 　 天氣陰
今天，媽媽說再過兩天，要帶我和弟弟
到外婆家玩，我和弟弟聽了好高興。

十月十七日 　 星期四 　 天气阴
今天，妈妈说再过两天，要带我和弟弟
到外婆家玩，我和弟弟听了好高兴。

Question 81

This is a

(A) letter to mother

(B) note to grandmother

(C) diary

(D) postcard

Question 82

When are they going to visit their grandmother?

(A) Thursday

(B) Friday

(C) Saturday

(D) Sunday

我今年十六歲，上十年級。我最喜歡的科目是體育，最討厭的科目是生物。每個星期除了上學，我還要練小提琴，到中文學校上課，每天只能睡五個小時。

我今年十六岁，上十年级。我最喜欢的科目是体育，最讨厌的科目是生物。每个星期除了上学，我还要练小提琴，到中文学校上课，每天只能睡五个小时。

Question 83   What grade am I now?

(A)   Freshman

(B)   Sophomore

(C)   Junior

(D)   Senior

Question 84   What is my favorite subject at school?

(A)   mathematics

(B)   chemistry

(C)   music

(D)   physical education

Question 85   What musical instrument do I play?

(A)   piano

(B)   harmonica

(C)   violin

(D)   cello

SAT II 中文模擬試題答案卷 - 第一套

Listening

1	Ⓐ	Ⓑ	Ⓒ	Ⓓ
2	Ⓐ	Ⓑ	Ⓒ	Ⓓ
3	Ⓐ	Ⓑ	Ⓒ	Ⓓ
4	Ⓐ	Ⓑ	Ⓒ	Ⓓ
5	Ⓐ	Ⓑ	Ⓒ	Ⓓ
6	Ⓐ	Ⓑ	Ⓒ	Ⓓ
7	Ⓐ	Ⓑ	Ⓒ	Ⓓ
8	Ⓐ	Ⓑ	Ⓒ	Ⓓ
9	Ⓐ	Ⓑ	Ⓒ	Ⓓ
10	Ⓐ	Ⓑ	Ⓒ	Ⓓ
11	Ⓐ	Ⓑ	Ⓒ	Ⓓ
12	Ⓐ	Ⓑ	Ⓒ	Ⓓ
13	Ⓐ	Ⓑ	Ⓒ	Ⓓ
14	Ⓐ	Ⓑ	Ⓒ	Ⓓ
15	Ⓐ	Ⓑ	Ⓒ	Ⓓ
16	Ⓐ	Ⓑ	Ⓒ	Ⓓ
17	Ⓐ	Ⓑ	Ⓒ	Ⓓ
18	Ⓐ	Ⓑ	Ⓒ	Ⓓ
19	Ⓐ	Ⓑ	Ⓒ	Ⓓ
20	Ⓐ	Ⓑ	Ⓒ	Ⓓ
21	Ⓐ	Ⓑ	Ⓒ	Ⓓ
22	Ⓐ	Ⓑ	Ⓒ	Ⓓ
23	Ⓐ	Ⓑ	Ⓒ	Ⓓ
24	Ⓐ	Ⓑ	Ⓒ	Ⓓ
25	Ⓐ	Ⓑ	Ⓒ	Ⓓ
26	Ⓐ	Ⓑ	Ⓒ	Ⓓ
27	Ⓐ	Ⓑ	Ⓒ	Ⓓ
28	Ⓐ	Ⓑ	Ⓒ	Ⓓ
29	Ⓐ	Ⓑ	Ⓒ	Ⓓ
30	Ⓐ	Ⓑ	Ⓒ	Ⓓ

Grammar

31	Ⓐ	Ⓑ	Ⓒ	Ⓓ
32	Ⓐ	Ⓑ	Ⓒ	Ⓓ
33	Ⓐ	Ⓑ	Ⓒ	Ⓓ
34	Ⓐ	Ⓑ	Ⓒ	Ⓓ
35	Ⓐ	Ⓑ	Ⓒ	Ⓓ
36	Ⓐ	Ⓑ	Ⓒ	Ⓓ
37	Ⓐ	Ⓑ	Ⓒ	Ⓓ
38	Ⓐ	Ⓑ	Ⓒ	Ⓓ
39	Ⓐ	Ⓑ	Ⓒ	Ⓓ
40	Ⓐ	Ⓑ	Ⓒ	Ⓓ
41	Ⓐ	Ⓑ	Ⓒ	Ⓓ
42	Ⓐ	Ⓑ	Ⓒ	Ⓓ
43	Ⓐ	Ⓑ	Ⓒ	Ⓓ
44	Ⓐ	Ⓑ	Ⓒ	Ⓓ
45	Ⓐ	Ⓑ	Ⓒ	Ⓓ
46	Ⓐ	Ⓑ	Ⓒ	Ⓓ
47	Ⓐ	Ⓑ	Ⓒ	Ⓓ
48	Ⓐ	Ⓑ	Ⓒ	Ⓓ
49	Ⓐ	Ⓑ	Ⓒ	Ⓓ
50	Ⓐ	Ⓑ	Ⓒ	Ⓓ
51	Ⓐ	Ⓑ	Ⓒ	Ⓓ
52	Ⓐ	Ⓑ	Ⓒ	Ⓓ
53	Ⓐ	Ⓑ	Ⓒ	Ⓓ
54	Ⓐ	Ⓑ	Ⓒ	Ⓓ
55	Ⓐ	Ⓑ	Ⓒ	Ⓓ

Reading

56	Ⓐ	Ⓑ	Ⓒ	Ⓓ
57	Ⓐ	Ⓑ	Ⓒ	Ⓓ
58	Ⓐ	Ⓑ	Ⓒ	Ⓓ
59	Ⓐ	Ⓑ	Ⓒ	Ⓓ
60	Ⓐ	Ⓑ	Ⓒ	Ⓓ
61	Ⓐ	Ⓑ	Ⓒ	Ⓓ
62	Ⓐ	Ⓑ	Ⓒ	Ⓓ
63	Ⓐ	Ⓑ	Ⓒ	Ⓓ
64	Ⓐ	Ⓑ	Ⓒ	Ⓓ
65	Ⓐ	Ⓑ	Ⓒ	Ⓓ
66	Ⓐ	Ⓑ	Ⓒ	Ⓓ
67	Ⓐ	Ⓑ	Ⓒ	Ⓓ
68	Ⓐ	Ⓑ	Ⓒ	Ⓓ
69	Ⓐ	Ⓑ	Ⓒ	Ⓓ
70	Ⓐ	Ⓑ	Ⓒ	Ⓓ
71	Ⓐ	Ⓑ	Ⓒ	Ⓓ
72	Ⓐ	Ⓑ	Ⓒ	Ⓓ
73	Ⓐ	Ⓑ	Ⓒ	Ⓓ
74	Ⓐ	Ⓑ	Ⓒ	Ⓓ
75	Ⓐ	Ⓑ	Ⓒ	Ⓓ
76	Ⓐ	Ⓑ	Ⓒ	Ⓓ
77	Ⓐ	Ⓑ	Ⓒ	Ⓓ
78	Ⓐ	Ⓑ	Ⓒ	Ⓓ
79	Ⓐ	Ⓑ	Ⓒ	Ⓓ
80	Ⓐ	Ⓑ	Ⓒ	Ⓓ
81	Ⓐ	Ⓑ	Ⓒ	Ⓓ
82	Ⓐ	Ⓑ	Ⓒ	Ⓓ
83	Ⓐ	Ⓑ	Ⓒ	Ⓓ
84	Ⓐ	Ⓑ	Ⓒ	Ⓓ
85	Ⓐ	Ⓑ	Ⓒ	Ⓓ

SAT II 中文模擬試題答案卷－第二套

Listening				
1	Ⓐ	Ⓑ	Ⓒ	Ⓓ
2	Ⓐ	Ⓑ	Ⓒ	Ⓓ
3	Ⓐ	Ⓑ	Ⓒ	Ⓓ
4	Ⓐ	Ⓑ	Ⓒ	Ⓓ
5	Ⓐ	Ⓑ	Ⓒ	Ⓓ
6	Ⓐ	Ⓑ	Ⓒ	Ⓓ
7	Ⓐ	Ⓑ	Ⓒ	Ⓓ
8	Ⓐ	Ⓑ	Ⓒ	Ⓓ
9	Ⓐ	Ⓑ	Ⓒ	Ⓓ
10	Ⓐ	Ⓑ	Ⓒ	Ⓓ
11	Ⓐ	Ⓑ	Ⓒ	Ⓓ
12	Ⓐ	Ⓑ	Ⓒ	Ⓓ
13	Ⓐ	Ⓑ	Ⓒ	Ⓓ
14	Ⓐ	Ⓑ	Ⓒ	Ⓓ
15	Ⓐ	Ⓑ	Ⓒ	Ⓓ
16	Ⓐ	Ⓑ	Ⓒ	Ⓓ
17	Ⓐ	Ⓑ	Ⓒ	Ⓓ
18	Ⓐ	Ⓑ	Ⓒ	Ⓓ
19	Ⓐ	Ⓑ	Ⓒ	Ⓓ
20	Ⓐ	Ⓑ	Ⓒ	Ⓓ
21	Ⓐ	Ⓑ	Ⓒ	Ⓓ
22	Ⓐ	Ⓑ	Ⓒ	Ⓓ
23	Ⓐ	Ⓑ	Ⓒ	Ⓓ
24	Ⓐ	Ⓑ	Ⓒ	Ⓓ
25	Ⓐ	Ⓑ	Ⓒ	Ⓓ
26	Ⓐ	Ⓑ	Ⓒ	Ⓓ
27	Ⓐ	Ⓑ	Ⓒ	Ⓓ
28	Ⓐ	Ⓑ	Ⓒ	Ⓓ
29	Ⓐ	Ⓑ	Ⓒ	Ⓓ
30	Ⓐ	Ⓑ	Ⓒ	Ⓓ

Grammar				
31	Ⓐ	Ⓑ	Ⓒ	Ⓓ
32	Ⓐ	Ⓑ	Ⓒ	Ⓓ
33	Ⓐ	Ⓑ	Ⓒ	Ⓓ
34	Ⓐ	Ⓑ	Ⓒ	Ⓓ
35	Ⓐ	Ⓑ	Ⓒ	Ⓓ
36	Ⓐ	Ⓑ	Ⓒ	Ⓓ
37	Ⓐ	Ⓑ	Ⓒ	Ⓓ
38	Ⓐ	Ⓑ	Ⓒ	Ⓓ
39	Ⓐ	Ⓑ	Ⓒ	Ⓓ
40	Ⓐ	Ⓑ	Ⓒ	Ⓓ
41	Ⓐ	Ⓑ	Ⓒ	Ⓓ
42	Ⓐ	Ⓑ	Ⓒ	Ⓓ
43	Ⓐ	Ⓑ	Ⓒ	Ⓓ
44	Ⓐ	Ⓑ	Ⓒ	Ⓓ
45	Ⓐ	Ⓑ	Ⓒ	Ⓓ
46	Ⓐ	Ⓑ	Ⓒ	Ⓓ
47	Ⓐ	Ⓑ	Ⓒ	Ⓓ
48	Ⓐ	Ⓑ	Ⓒ	Ⓓ
49	Ⓐ	Ⓑ	Ⓒ	Ⓓ
50	Ⓐ	Ⓑ	Ⓒ	Ⓓ
51	Ⓐ	Ⓑ	Ⓒ	Ⓓ
52	Ⓐ	Ⓑ	Ⓒ	Ⓓ
53	Ⓐ	Ⓑ	Ⓒ	Ⓓ
54	Ⓐ	Ⓑ	Ⓒ	Ⓓ
55	Ⓐ	Ⓑ	Ⓒ	Ⓓ

Reading				
56	Ⓐ	Ⓑ	Ⓒ	Ⓓ
57	Ⓐ	Ⓑ	Ⓒ	Ⓓ
58	Ⓐ	Ⓑ	Ⓒ	Ⓓ
59	Ⓐ	Ⓑ	Ⓒ	Ⓓ
60	Ⓐ	Ⓑ	Ⓒ	Ⓓ
61	Ⓐ	Ⓑ	Ⓒ	Ⓓ
62	Ⓐ	Ⓑ	Ⓒ	Ⓓ
63	Ⓐ	Ⓑ	Ⓒ	Ⓓ
64	Ⓐ	Ⓑ	Ⓒ	Ⓓ
65	Ⓐ	Ⓑ	Ⓒ	Ⓓ
66	Ⓐ	Ⓑ	Ⓒ	Ⓓ
67	Ⓐ	Ⓑ	Ⓒ	Ⓓ
68	Ⓐ	Ⓑ	Ⓒ	Ⓓ
69	Ⓐ	Ⓑ	Ⓒ	Ⓓ
70	Ⓐ	Ⓑ	Ⓒ	Ⓓ
71	Ⓐ	Ⓑ	Ⓒ	Ⓓ
72	Ⓐ	Ⓑ	Ⓒ	Ⓓ
73	Ⓐ	Ⓑ	Ⓒ	Ⓓ
74	Ⓐ	Ⓑ	Ⓒ	Ⓓ
75	Ⓐ	Ⓑ	Ⓒ	Ⓓ
76	Ⓐ	Ⓑ	Ⓒ	Ⓓ
77	Ⓐ	Ⓑ	Ⓒ	Ⓓ
78	Ⓐ	Ⓑ	Ⓒ	Ⓓ
79	Ⓐ	Ⓑ	Ⓒ	Ⓓ
80	Ⓐ	Ⓑ	Ⓒ	Ⓓ
81	Ⓐ	Ⓑ	Ⓒ	Ⓓ
82	Ⓐ	Ⓑ	Ⓒ	Ⓓ
83	Ⓐ	Ⓑ	Ⓒ	Ⓓ
84	Ⓐ	Ⓑ	Ⓒ	Ⓓ
85	Ⓐ	Ⓑ	Ⓒ	Ⓓ

SAT II 中文模擬試題答案卷 - 第三套

Listening	Grammar	Reading
1 Ⓐ Ⓑ Ⓒ Ⓓ	31 Ⓐ Ⓑ Ⓒ Ⓓ	56 Ⓐ Ⓑ Ⓒ Ⓓ
2 Ⓐ Ⓑ Ⓒ Ⓓ	32 Ⓐ Ⓑ Ⓒ Ⓓ	57 Ⓐ Ⓑ Ⓒ Ⓓ
3 Ⓐ Ⓑ Ⓒ Ⓓ	33 Ⓐ Ⓑ Ⓒ Ⓓ	58 Ⓐ Ⓑ Ⓒ Ⓓ
4 Ⓐ Ⓑ Ⓒ Ⓓ	34 Ⓐ Ⓑ Ⓒ Ⓓ	59 Ⓐ Ⓑ Ⓒ Ⓓ
5 Ⓐ Ⓑ Ⓒ Ⓓ	35 Ⓐ Ⓑ Ⓒ Ⓓ	60 Ⓐ Ⓑ Ⓒ Ⓓ
6 Ⓐ Ⓑ Ⓒ Ⓓ	36 Ⓐ Ⓑ Ⓒ Ⓓ	61 Ⓐ Ⓑ Ⓒ Ⓓ
7 Ⓐ Ⓑ Ⓒ Ⓓ	37 Ⓐ Ⓑ Ⓒ Ⓓ	62 Ⓐ Ⓑ Ⓒ Ⓓ
8 Ⓐ Ⓑ Ⓒ Ⓓ	38 Ⓐ Ⓑ Ⓒ Ⓓ	63 Ⓐ Ⓑ Ⓒ Ⓓ
9 Ⓐ Ⓑ Ⓒ Ⓓ	39 Ⓐ Ⓑ Ⓒ Ⓓ	64 Ⓐ Ⓑ Ⓒ Ⓓ
10 Ⓐ Ⓑ Ⓒ Ⓓ	40 Ⓐ Ⓑ Ⓒ Ⓓ	65 Ⓐ Ⓑ Ⓒ Ⓓ
11 Ⓐ Ⓑ Ⓒ Ⓓ	41 Ⓐ Ⓑ Ⓒ Ⓓ	66 Ⓐ Ⓑ Ⓒ Ⓓ
12 Ⓐ Ⓑ Ⓒ Ⓓ	42 Ⓐ Ⓑ Ⓒ Ⓓ	67 Ⓐ Ⓑ Ⓒ Ⓓ
13 Ⓐ Ⓑ Ⓒ Ⓓ	43 Ⓐ Ⓑ Ⓒ Ⓓ	68 Ⓐ Ⓑ Ⓒ Ⓓ
14 Ⓐ Ⓑ Ⓒ Ⓓ	44 Ⓐ Ⓑ Ⓒ Ⓓ	69 Ⓐ Ⓑ Ⓒ Ⓓ
15 Ⓐ Ⓑ Ⓒ Ⓓ	45 Ⓐ Ⓑ Ⓒ Ⓓ	70 Ⓐ Ⓑ Ⓒ Ⓓ
16 Ⓐ Ⓑ Ⓒ Ⓓ	46 Ⓐ Ⓑ Ⓒ Ⓓ	71 Ⓐ Ⓑ Ⓒ Ⓓ
17 Ⓐ Ⓑ Ⓒ Ⓓ	47 Ⓐ Ⓑ Ⓒ Ⓓ	72 Ⓐ Ⓑ Ⓒ Ⓓ
18 Ⓐ Ⓑ Ⓒ Ⓓ	48 Ⓐ Ⓑ Ⓒ Ⓓ	73 Ⓐ Ⓑ Ⓒ Ⓓ
19 Ⓐ Ⓑ Ⓒ Ⓓ	49 Ⓐ Ⓑ Ⓒ Ⓓ	74 Ⓐ Ⓑ Ⓒ Ⓓ
20 Ⓐ Ⓑ Ⓒ Ⓓ	50 Ⓐ Ⓑ Ⓒ Ⓓ	75 Ⓐ Ⓑ Ⓒ Ⓓ
21 Ⓐ Ⓑ Ⓒ Ⓓ	51 Ⓐ Ⓑ Ⓒ Ⓓ	76 Ⓐ Ⓑ Ⓒ Ⓓ
22 Ⓐ Ⓑ Ⓒ Ⓓ	52 Ⓐ Ⓑ Ⓒ Ⓓ	77 Ⓐ Ⓑ Ⓒ Ⓓ
23 Ⓐ Ⓑ Ⓒ Ⓓ	53 Ⓐ Ⓑ Ⓒ Ⓓ	78 Ⓐ Ⓑ Ⓒ Ⓓ
24 Ⓐ Ⓑ Ⓒ Ⓓ	54 Ⓐ Ⓑ Ⓒ Ⓓ	79 Ⓐ Ⓑ Ⓒ Ⓓ
25 Ⓐ Ⓑ Ⓒ Ⓓ	55 Ⓐ Ⓑ Ⓒ Ⓓ	80 Ⓐ Ⓑ Ⓒ Ⓓ
26 Ⓐ Ⓑ Ⓒ Ⓓ		81 Ⓐ Ⓑ Ⓒ Ⓓ
27 Ⓐ Ⓑ Ⓒ Ⓓ		82 Ⓐ Ⓑ Ⓒ Ⓓ
28 Ⓐ Ⓑ Ⓒ Ⓓ		83 Ⓐ Ⓑ Ⓒ Ⓓ
29 Ⓐ Ⓑ Ⓒ Ⓓ		84 Ⓐ Ⓑ Ⓒ Ⓓ
30 Ⓐ Ⓑ Ⓒ Ⓓ		85 Ⓐ Ⓑ Ⓒ Ⓓ

SAT II 中文模擬試題答案卷 - 第四套

Listening	Grammar	Reading
1 Ⓐ Ⓑ Ⓒ Ⓓ	31 Ⓐ Ⓑ Ⓒ Ⓓ	56 Ⓐ Ⓑ Ⓒ Ⓓ
2 Ⓐ Ⓑ Ⓒ Ⓓ	32 Ⓐ Ⓑ Ⓒ Ⓓ	57 Ⓐ Ⓑ Ⓒ Ⓓ
3 Ⓐ Ⓑ Ⓒ Ⓓ	33 Ⓐ Ⓑ Ⓒ Ⓓ	58 Ⓐ Ⓑ Ⓒ Ⓓ
4 Ⓐ Ⓑ Ⓒ Ⓓ	34 Ⓐ Ⓑ Ⓒ Ⓓ	59 Ⓐ Ⓑ Ⓒ Ⓓ
5 Ⓐ Ⓑ Ⓒ Ⓓ	35 Ⓐ Ⓑ Ⓒ Ⓓ	60 Ⓐ Ⓑ Ⓒ Ⓓ
6 Ⓐ Ⓑ Ⓒ Ⓓ	36 Ⓐ Ⓑ Ⓒ Ⓓ	61 Ⓐ Ⓑ Ⓒ Ⓓ
7 Ⓐ Ⓑ Ⓒ Ⓓ	37 Ⓐ Ⓑ Ⓒ Ⓓ	62 Ⓐ Ⓑ Ⓒ Ⓓ
8 Ⓐ Ⓑ Ⓒ Ⓓ	38 Ⓐ Ⓑ Ⓒ Ⓓ	63 Ⓐ Ⓑ Ⓒ Ⓓ
9 Ⓐ Ⓑ Ⓒ Ⓓ	39 Ⓐ Ⓑ Ⓒ Ⓓ	64 Ⓐ Ⓑ Ⓒ Ⓓ
10 Ⓐ Ⓑ Ⓒ Ⓓ	40 Ⓐ Ⓑ Ⓒ Ⓓ	65 Ⓐ Ⓑ Ⓒ Ⓓ
11 Ⓐ Ⓑ Ⓒ Ⓓ	41 Ⓐ Ⓑ Ⓒ Ⓓ	66 Ⓐ Ⓑ Ⓒ Ⓓ
12 Ⓐ Ⓑ Ⓒ Ⓓ	42 Ⓐ Ⓑ Ⓒ Ⓓ	67 Ⓐ Ⓑ Ⓒ Ⓓ
13 Ⓐ Ⓑ Ⓒ Ⓓ	43 Ⓐ Ⓑ Ⓒ Ⓓ	68 Ⓐ Ⓑ Ⓒ Ⓓ
14 Ⓐ Ⓑ Ⓒ Ⓓ	44 Ⓐ Ⓑ Ⓒ Ⓓ	69 Ⓐ Ⓑ Ⓒ Ⓓ
15 Ⓐ Ⓑ Ⓒ Ⓓ	45 Ⓐ Ⓑ Ⓒ Ⓓ	70 Ⓐ Ⓑ Ⓒ Ⓓ
16 Ⓐ Ⓑ Ⓒ Ⓓ	46 Ⓐ Ⓑ Ⓒ Ⓓ	71 Ⓐ Ⓑ Ⓒ Ⓓ
17 Ⓐ Ⓑ Ⓒ Ⓓ	47 Ⓐ Ⓑ Ⓒ Ⓓ	72 Ⓐ Ⓑ Ⓒ Ⓓ
18 Ⓐ Ⓑ Ⓒ Ⓓ	48 Ⓐ Ⓑ Ⓒ Ⓓ	73 Ⓐ Ⓑ Ⓒ Ⓓ
19 Ⓐ Ⓑ Ⓒ Ⓓ	49 Ⓐ Ⓑ Ⓒ Ⓓ	74 Ⓐ Ⓑ Ⓒ Ⓓ
20 Ⓐ Ⓑ Ⓒ Ⓓ	50 Ⓐ Ⓑ Ⓒ Ⓓ	75 Ⓐ Ⓑ Ⓒ Ⓓ
21 Ⓐ Ⓑ Ⓒ Ⓓ	51 Ⓐ Ⓑ Ⓒ Ⓓ	76 Ⓐ Ⓑ Ⓒ Ⓓ
22 Ⓐ Ⓑ Ⓒ Ⓓ	52 Ⓐ Ⓑ Ⓒ Ⓓ	77 Ⓐ Ⓑ Ⓒ Ⓓ
23 Ⓐ Ⓑ Ⓒ Ⓓ	53 Ⓐ Ⓑ Ⓒ Ⓓ	78 Ⓐ Ⓑ Ⓒ Ⓓ
24 Ⓐ Ⓑ Ⓒ Ⓓ	54 Ⓐ Ⓑ Ⓒ Ⓓ	79 Ⓐ Ⓑ Ⓒ Ⓓ
25 Ⓐ Ⓑ Ⓒ Ⓓ	55 Ⓐ Ⓑ Ⓒ Ⓓ	80 Ⓐ Ⓑ Ⓒ Ⓓ
26 Ⓐ Ⓑ Ⓒ Ⓓ		81 Ⓐ Ⓑ Ⓒ Ⓓ
27 Ⓐ Ⓑ Ⓒ Ⓓ		82 Ⓐ Ⓑ Ⓒ Ⓓ
28 Ⓐ Ⓑ Ⓒ Ⓓ		83 Ⓐ Ⓑ Ⓒ Ⓓ
29 Ⓐ Ⓑ Ⓒ Ⓓ		84 Ⓐ Ⓑ Ⓒ Ⓓ
30 Ⓐ Ⓑ Ⓒ Ⓓ		85 Ⓐ Ⓑ Ⓒ Ⓓ

SAT II 中文模擬試題答案卷 - 第五套

Listening	Grammar	Reading
1 (A) (B) (C) (D)	31 (A) (B) (C) (D)	56 (A) (B) (C) (D)
2 (A) (B) (C) (D)	32 (A) (B) (C) (D)	57 (A) (B) (C) (D)
3 (A) (B) (C) (D)	33 (A) (B) (C) (D)	58 (A) (B) (C) (D)
4 (A) (B) (C) (D)	34 (A) (B) (C) (D)	59 (A) (B) (C) (D)
5 (A) (B) (C) (D)	35 (A) (B) (C) (D)	60 (A) (B) (C) (D)
6 (A) (B) (C) (D)	36 (A) (B) (C) (D)	61 (A) (B) (C) (D)
7 (A) (B) (C) (D)	37 (A) (B) (C) (D)	62 (A) (B) (C) (D)
8 (A) (B) (C) (D)	38 (A) (B) (C) (D)	63 (A) (B) (C) (D)
9 (A) (B) (C) (D)	39 (A) (B) (C) (D)	64 (A) (B) (C) (D)
10 (A) (B) (C) (D)	40 (A) (B) (C) (D)	65 (A) (B) (C) (D)
11 (A) (B) (C) (D)	41 (A) (B) (C) (D)	66 (A) (B) (C) (D)
12 (A) (B) (C) (D)	42 (A) (B) (C) (D)	67 (A) (B) (C) (D)
13 (A) (B) (C) (D)	43 (A) (B) (C) (D)	68 (A) (B) (C) (D)
14 (A) (B) (C) (D)	44 (A) (B) (C) (D)	69 (A) (B) (C) (D)
15 (A) (B) (C) (D)	45 (A) (B) (C) (D)	70 (A) (B) (C) (D)
16 (A) (B) (C) (D)	46 (A) (B) (C) (D)	71 (A) (B) (C) (D)
17 (A) (B) (C) (D)	47 (A) (B) (C) (D)	72 (A) (B) (C) (D)
18 (A) (B) (C) (D)	48 (A) (B) (C) (D)	73 (A) (B) (C) (D)
19 (A) (B) (C) (D)	49 (A) (B) (C) (D)	74 (A) (B) (C) (D)
20 (A) (B) (C) (D)	50 (A) (B) (C) (D)	75 (A) (B) (C) (D)
21 (A) (B) (C) (D)	51 (A) (B) (C) (D)	76 (A) (B) (C) (D)
22 (A) (B) (C) (D)	52 (A) (B) (C) (D)	77 (A) (B) (C) (D)
23 (A) (B) (C) (D)	53 (A) (B) (C) (D)	78 (A) (B) (C) (D)
24 (A) (B) (C) (D)	54 (A) (B) (C) (D)	79 (A) (B) (C) (D)
25 (A) (B) (C) (D)	55 (A) (B) (C) (D)	80 (A) (B) (C) (D)
26 (A) (B) (C) (D)		81 (A) (B) (C) (D)
27 (A) (B) (C) (D)		82 (A) (B) (C) (D)
28 (A) (B) (C) (D)		83 (A) (B) (C) (D)
29 (A) (B) (C) (D)		84 (A) (B) (C) (D)
30 (A) (B) (C) (D)		85 (A) (B) (C) (D)

SAT II 中文模擬試題答案卷 - 第六套

Listening

1 Ⓐ Ⓑ Ⓒ Ⓓ
2 Ⓐ Ⓑ Ⓒ Ⓓ
3 Ⓐ Ⓑ Ⓒ Ⓓ
4 Ⓐ Ⓑ Ⓒ Ⓓ
5 Ⓐ Ⓑ Ⓒ Ⓓ

6 Ⓐ Ⓑ Ⓒ Ⓓ
7 Ⓐ Ⓑ Ⓒ Ⓓ
8 Ⓐ Ⓑ Ⓒ Ⓓ
9 Ⓐ Ⓑ Ⓒ Ⓓ
10 Ⓐ Ⓑ Ⓒ Ⓓ

11 Ⓐ Ⓑ Ⓒ Ⓓ
12 Ⓐ Ⓑ Ⓒ Ⓓ
13 Ⓐ Ⓑ Ⓒ Ⓓ
14 Ⓐ Ⓑ Ⓒ Ⓓ
15 Ⓐ Ⓑ Ⓒ Ⓓ

16 Ⓐ Ⓑ Ⓒ Ⓓ
17 Ⓐ Ⓑ Ⓒ Ⓓ
18 Ⓐ Ⓑ Ⓒ Ⓓ
19 Ⓐ Ⓑ Ⓒ Ⓓ
20 Ⓐ Ⓑ Ⓒ Ⓓ

21 Ⓐ Ⓑ Ⓒ Ⓓ
22 Ⓐ Ⓑ Ⓒ Ⓓ
23 Ⓐ Ⓑ Ⓒ Ⓓ
24 Ⓐ Ⓑ Ⓒ Ⓓ
25 Ⓐ Ⓑ Ⓒ Ⓓ

26 Ⓐ Ⓑ Ⓒ Ⓓ
27 Ⓐ Ⓑ Ⓒ Ⓓ
28 Ⓐ Ⓑ Ⓒ Ⓓ
29 Ⓐ Ⓑ Ⓒ Ⓓ
30 Ⓐ Ⓑ Ⓒ Ⓓ

Grammar

31 Ⓐ Ⓑ Ⓒ Ⓓ
32 Ⓐ Ⓑ Ⓒ Ⓓ
33 Ⓐ Ⓑ Ⓒ Ⓓ
34 Ⓐ Ⓑ Ⓒ Ⓓ
35 Ⓐ Ⓑ Ⓒ Ⓓ

36 Ⓐ Ⓑ Ⓒ Ⓓ
37 Ⓐ Ⓑ Ⓒ Ⓓ
38 Ⓐ Ⓑ Ⓒ Ⓓ
39 Ⓐ Ⓑ Ⓒ Ⓓ
40 Ⓐ Ⓑ Ⓒ Ⓓ

41 Ⓐ Ⓑ Ⓒ Ⓓ
42 Ⓐ Ⓑ Ⓒ Ⓓ
43 Ⓐ Ⓑ Ⓒ Ⓓ
44 Ⓐ Ⓑ Ⓒ Ⓓ
45 Ⓐ Ⓑ Ⓒ Ⓓ

46 Ⓐ Ⓑ Ⓒ Ⓓ
47 Ⓐ Ⓑ Ⓒ Ⓓ
48 Ⓐ Ⓑ Ⓒ Ⓓ
49 Ⓐ Ⓑ Ⓒ Ⓓ
50 Ⓐ Ⓑ Ⓒ Ⓓ

51 Ⓐ Ⓑ Ⓒ Ⓓ
52 Ⓐ Ⓑ Ⓒ Ⓓ
53 Ⓐ Ⓑ Ⓒ Ⓓ
54 Ⓐ Ⓑ Ⓒ Ⓓ
55 Ⓐ Ⓑ Ⓒ Ⓓ

Reading

56 Ⓐ Ⓑ Ⓒ Ⓓ
57 Ⓐ Ⓑ Ⓒ Ⓓ
58 Ⓐ Ⓑ Ⓒ Ⓓ
59 Ⓐ Ⓑ Ⓒ Ⓓ
60 Ⓐ Ⓑ Ⓒ Ⓓ

61 Ⓐ Ⓑ Ⓒ Ⓓ
62 Ⓐ Ⓑ Ⓒ Ⓓ
63 Ⓐ Ⓑ Ⓒ Ⓓ
64 Ⓐ Ⓑ Ⓒ Ⓓ
65 Ⓐ Ⓑ Ⓒ Ⓓ

66 Ⓐ Ⓑ Ⓒ Ⓓ
67 Ⓐ Ⓑ Ⓒ Ⓓ
68 Ⓐ Ⓑ Ⓒ Ⓓ
69 Ⓐ Ⓑ Ⓒ Ⓓ
70 Ⓐ Ⓑ Ⓒ Ⓓ

71 Ⓐ Ⓑ Ⓒ Ⓓ
72 Ⓐ Ⓑ Ⓒ Ⓓ
73 Ⓐ Ⓑ Ⓒ Ⓓ
74 Ⓐ Ⓑ Ⓒ Ⓓ
75 Ⓐ Ⓑ Ⓒ Ⓓ

76 Ⓐ Ⓑ Ⓒ Ⓓ
77 Ⓐ Ⓑ Ⓒ Ⓓ
78 Ⓐ Ⓑ Ⓒ Ⓓ
79 Ⓐ Ⓑ Ⓒ Ⓓ
80 Ⓐ Ⓑ Ⓒ Ⓓ

81 Ⓐ Ⓑ Ⓒ Ⓓ
82 Ⓐ Ⓑ Ⓒ Ⓓ
83 Ⓐ Ⓑ Ⓒ Ⓓ
84 Ⓐ Ⓑ Ⓒ Ⓓ
85 Ⓐ Ⓑ Ⓒ Ⓓ

SAT II 中文模擬試題答案 - 第一套

Listening		Grammar		Reading	
1	**A** B C D	31	A B **C** D	56	A B **C** D
2	A **B** C D	32	A B **C** D	57	A **B** C D
3	A B **C** D	33	**A** B C D	58	A B C **D**
4	A B **C** D	34	A B **C** D	59	A **B** C D
5	**A** B C D	35	A B **C** D	60	A B C **D**
6	A B **C** D	36	A B **C** D	61	A **B** C D
7	A **B** C D	37	A **B** C D	62	A **B** C D
8	A B **C** D	38	A B **C** D	63	**A** B C D
9	A B **C** D	39	A **B** C D	64	**A** B C D
10	A B **C** D	40	A **B** C D	65	A B C **D**
11	**A** B C D	41	A B **C** D	66	A **B** C D
12	A **B** C D	42	A **B** C D	67	**A** B C D
13	A **B** C D	43	A B C **D**	68	A **B** C D
14	A **B** C D	44	A B **C** D	69	**A** B C D
15	**A** B C D	45	A **B** C D	70	A B **C** D
16	**A** B C D	46	A B **C** D	71	**A** B C D
17	A B **C** D	47	A B **C** D	72	A B **C** D
18	**A** B C D	48	A **B** C D	73	A **B** C D
19	A B **C** D	49	A B C **D**	74	A **B** C D
20	**A** B C D	50	A **B** C D	75	**A** B C D
21	A B **C** D	51	A B C **D**	76	A B C **D**
22	A B **C** D	52	A B C **D**	77	A B **C** D
23	A **B** C D	53	A B C **D**	78	A B **C** D
24	A **B** C D	54	A B **C** D	79	A **B** C D
25	A **B** C D	55	**A** B C D	80	**A** B C D
26	A B **C** D			81	**A** B C D
27	A B C **D**			82	A B **C** D
28	A B C **D**			83	A B C **D**
29	A B C **D**			84	**A** B C D
30	A B **C** D			85	A B **C** D

SAT II 中文模擬試題答案-第二套

Listening				
1	A	**B**	C	D
2	A	**B**	C	D
3	A	B	**C**	D
4	**A**	B	C	D
5	**A**	B	C	D
6	A	**B**	C	D
7	**A**	B	C	D
8	**A**	B	C	D
9	A	**B**	C	D
10	A	**B**	C	D
11	A	**B**	C	D
12	A	B	**C**	D
13	A	**B**	C	D
14	**A**	B	C	D
15	A	**B**	C	D
16	A	B	**C**	D
17	A	B	**C**	D
18	A	B	C	**D**
19	A	**B**	C	D
20	**A**	B	C	D
21	A	**B**	C	D
22	**A**	B	C	D
23	**A**	B	C	D
24	A	B	**C**	D
25	A	B	**C**	D
26	A	B	C	**D**
27	A	B	**C**	D
28	**A**	B	C	D
29	A	B	C	**D**
30	A	B	**C**	D

Grammar				
31	A	B	C	**D**
32	**A**	B	C	D
33	A	**B**	C	D
34	A	B	C	**D**
35	A	**B**	C	D
36	A	B	**C**	D
37	A	B	C	**D**
38	**A**	B	C	D
39	**A**	B	C	D
40	**A**	B	C	D
41	A	**B**	C	D
42	A	**B**	C	D
43	A	B	C	**D**
44	A	**B**	C	D
45	**A**	B	C	D
46	A	B	**C**	D
47	A	B	**C**	D
48	A	B	**C**	D
49	A	B	**C**	D
50	**A**	B	C	D
51	A	B	**C**	D
52	A	B	**C**	D
53	A	**B**	C	D
54	A	**B**	C	D
55	**A**	B	C	D

Reading				
56	A	B	C	**D**
57	A	B	**C**	D
58	A	**B**	C	D
59	**A**	B	C	D
60	A	B	C	**D**
61	A	B	**C**	D
62	A	**B**	C	D
63	**A**	B	C	D
64	**A**	B	C	D
65	A	**B**	C	D
66	A	B	C	**D**
67	**A**	B	C	D
68	A	B	**C**	D
69	A	**B**	C	D
70	A	B	C	**D**
71	A	B	C	**D**
72	A	B	**C**	D
73	A	B	C	**D**
74	A	B	**C**	D
75	A	B	**C**	D
76	A	B	C	**D**
77	A	**B**	C	D
78	A	**B**	C	D
79	A	**B**	C	D
80	A	B	**C**	D
81	A	B	**C**	D
82	A	B	C	**D**
83	A	B	C	**D**
84	A	B	**C**	D
85	A	**B**	C	D

SAT II 中文模擬試題答案 - 第三套

Listening	Grammar	Reading
1. A	31. B	56. A
2. B	32. B	57. B
3. B	33. D	58. D
4. B	34. C	59. C
5. B	35. C	60. A
6. C	36. C	61. B
7. C	37. D	62. A
8. C	38. C	63. B
9. A	39. C	64. C
10. A	40. B	65. B
11. B	41. C	66. C
12. B	42. C	67. C
13. A	43. B	68. A
14. B	44. B	69. B
15. A	45. A	70. D
16. A	46. C	71. D
17. D	47. B	72. B
18. C	48. B	73. C
19. D	49. C	74. B
20. A	50. B	75. B
21. C	51. C	76. D
22. D	52. C	77. A
23. B	53. A	78. B
24. C	54. B	79. A
25. C	55. C	80. B
26. A		81. B
27. B		82. D
28. D		83. A
29. B		84. B
30. C		85. B

SAT II 中文模擬試題答案 - 第四套

Listening				
1	A	B	**C**	D
2	A	**B**	C	D
3	A	**B**	C	D
4	A	**B**	C	D
5	A	B	**C**	D
6	A	B	**C**	D
7	A	**B**	C	D
8	A	**B**	C	D
9	**A**	B	C	D
10	A	B	**C**	D
11	A	B	**C**	D
12	**A**	B	C	D
13	A	B	**C**	D
14	A	**B**	C	D
15	**A**	B	C	D
16	A	B	C	**D**
17	A	B	**C**	D
18	A	**B**	C	D
19	A	B	C	**D**
20	**A**	B	C	D
21	A	B	C	**D**
22	A	**B**	C	D
23	**A**	B	C	D
24	A	B	C	**D**
25	A	**B**	C	D
26	A	B	C	**D**
27	A	**B**	C	D
28	**A**	B	C	D
29	A	B	**C**	D
30	A	B	**C**	D

Grammar				
31	A	**B**	C	D
32	**A**	B	C	D
33	A	**B**	C	D
34	A	**B**	C	D
35	A	B	**C**	D
36	**A**	B	C	D
37	**A**	B	C	D
38	A	B	**C**	D
39	A	B	**C**	D
40	A	B	**C**	D
41	A	B	C	**D**
42	**A**	B	C	D
43	A	B	**C**	D
44	**A**	B	C	D
45	A	B	C	**D**
46	A	B	C	**D**
47	A	**B**	C	D
48	A	**B**	C	D
49	**A**	B	C	D
50	A	B	C	**D**
51	A	B	**C**	D
52	A	B	**C**	D
53	A	B	**C**	D
54	A	B	C	**D**
55	A	**B**	C	D

Reading				
56	A	**B**	C	D
57	A	B	C	**D**
58	A	**B**	C	D
59	A	B	**C**	D
60	A	B	**C**	D
61	A	B	**C**	D
62	**A**	B	C	D
63	**A**	B	C	D
64	A	B	C	**D**
65	A	B	**C**	D
66	A	**B**	C	D
67	A	B	**C**	D
68	A	B	**C**	D
69	**A**	B	C	D
70	A	**B**	C	D
71	A	B	C	**D**
72	A	B	C	**D**
73	A	B	**C**	D
74	A	B	C	**D**
75	A	B	**C**	D
76	A	B	C	**D**
77	A	B	**C**	D
78	A	B	C	**D**
79	**A**	B	C	D
80	A	B	C	**D**
81	A	B	**C**	D
82	**A**	B	C	D
83	A	**B**	C	D
84	A	**B**	C	D
85	A	B	C	**D**

SAT II 中文模擬試題答案 - 第五套

Listening	Grammar	Reading
1 B	31 D	56 C
2 C	32 A	57 C
3 B	33 D	58 B
4 C	34 A	59 D
5 C	35 A	60 A
6 A	36 D	61 B
7 A	37 C	62 A
8 B	38 C	63 C
9 C	39 B	64 D
10 C	40 B	65 D
11 C	41 C	66 C
12 B	42 C	67 A
13 B	43 D	68 D
14 A	44 D	69 A
15 C	45 D	70 B
16 B	46 C	71 C
17 B	47 D	72 D
18 B	48 D	73 C
19 D	49 C	74 B
20 B	50 B	75 C
21 A	51 D	76 D
22 B	52 D	77 C
23 A	53 C	78 B
24 C	54 C	79 D
25 A	55 C	80 B
26 D		81 C
27 A		82 B
28 D		83 D
29 D		84 C
30 C		85 B

SAT II 中文模擬試題答案 - 第六套

Listening	Grammar	Reading
1. A B **C** D	31. A **B** C D	56. A B **C** D
2. A B **C** D	32. A B **C** D	57. A **B** C D
3. **A** B C D	33. A B **C** D	58. A B C **D**
4. A B **C** D	34. **A** B C D	59. **A** B C D
5. A **B** C D	35. **A** B C D	60. A B **C** D
6. A B **C** D	36. **A** B C D	61. A B **C** D
7. A B **C** D	37. A **B** C D	62. A B **C** D
8. **A** B C D	38. A B C **D**	63. A **B** C D
9. A B **C** D	39. **A** B C D	64. A B C **D**
10. A B **C** D	40. A B C **D**	65. A **B** C D
11. A **B** C D	41. A B **C** D	66. A B **C** D
12. A B **C** D	42. **A** B C D	67. **A** B C D
13. A B **C** D	43. A B C **D**	68. **A** B C D
14. **A** B C D	44. **A** B C D	69. A B C **D**
15. A **B** C D	45. A **B** C D	70. A **B** C D
16. **A** B C D	46. A B C **D**	71. A **B** C D
17. **A** B C D	47. A **B** C D	72. A B **C** D
18. **A** B C D	48. A **B** C D	73. **A** B C D
19. **A** B C D	49. A B C **D**	74. A B **C** D
20. A B **C** D	50. A B **C** D	75. A B C **D**
21. A B **C** D	51. A B **C** D	76. A B **C** D
22. A **B** C D	52. A **B** C D	77. A **B** C D
23. A **B** C D	53. A B **C** D	78. A **B** C D
24. **A** B C D	54. A B C **D**	79. A B **C** D
25. A B C **D**	55. A B C **D**	80. **A** B C D
26. **A** B C D		81. A B **C** D
27. A B **C** D		82. A B **C** D
28. A **B** C D		83. A **B** C D
29. A **B** C D		84. A B C **D**
30. A **B** C D		85. A B **C** D

【編者註】

- 本書六套模擬考題，Section II 文法的漢語拼音部份，爲配合注音符號的拼音模式，均採用單字拼音法，只有人名與地名，依照慣用的詞語拼法。

- 參與本書編輯的老師及工作人員均屬義工，本書之專業表達若有疏漏之處，歡迎指正，並請包涵，謝謝！

編輯室 敬啟

- 本书六套模拟考题，Section II 文法的汉语拼音部份，为配合注音符号的拼音模式，均採用单字拼音法，只有人名与地名，依照惯用的词语拼法。

- 参与本书编辑的老师及工作人员均属义工，本书之专业表达若有疏漏之处，欢迎指正，並请包涵，谢谢！

编辑室 敬启